In honor of
HERMAN A. and
RUTH H. UTTER

GOT TO
GIVE THE PEOPLE
WHAT THEY
WANT

GOT TO GIVE THE PEOPLE WHAT THEY WANT

True Stories

and

Flagrant Opinions

from

Center Court

JALEN ROSE

Crown Archetype
NEW YORK

All rights reserved.
Published in the United States by Crown Archetype, an imprint of the
Crown Publishing Group, a division of Penguin Random House LLC, New York.
www.crownpublishing.com

CROWN ARCHETYPE and colophon is a registered trademark of
Penguin Random House LLC.

Library of Congress Cataloging-in-Publication Data is available upon request.

ISBN 978-0-8041-3890-1
eBook ISBN 978-0-8041-3891-8

Printed in the United States of America

Jacket design by Elena Giavaldi
Jacket lettering by Luca Barcellona
Jacket photograph by Zach Cordner

10 9 8 7 6 5 4 3 2 1

First Edition

With love and humble thanks

to my ma and grammie

for teaching me how to be a man.

Failure was never an option!

CONTENTS

FOREWORD BY BILL SIMMONS

In February of 2014, Jalen Rose and I were in New Orleans for NBA All-Star Weekend. Jalen had just turned forty-one, so we taped our *NBA Countdown* show and headed out for a belated birthday dinner in the French Quarter. I ordered a Moscow Mule (vodka, ginger beer, and lime), which arrived in a fancy copper mug. Jalen had already gotten wine, but he became jealous of my special mug and ordered one, too. (Just like that, Jalen had a new favorite drink. He's that easy.) He also requested a well-done lobster for his entrée, which happens at every nice Jalen dinner for three reasons: First, he loves lobster, but doesn't like when it's squishy. Second, he grew up in Detroit with absolutely nothing, about as poor as a little kid can possibly be, which continued to be the case even after the Fab Five started printing millions for Michigan (Jalen and his teammates weren't seeing a dime). You know what Jalen Rose wasn't seeing a lot of from age one to age twenty? Lobster. You don't have to be a psychology major to understand the symbolism there; even Jalen admits as much. He ended up playing in the NBA for thirteen years. At some point—and he doesn't remember exactly when—he could afford fancy dinners, and he could afford the freaking lobster. Well done. Or he's sending it back like Mutombo.

Jalen is a creature of habit. He orders the same entrées and drinks and junk-food items. He haunts the same eating and drinking establishments. He falls asleep on airplanes during the exact same time (about five minutes before it takes off) and wakes up during the exact same time (right before it lands). There are thirty funnier things that I wish I could list (but can't). Maybe for the next book. He's the most unpredictably predictable friend I ever had. And that French Quarter dinner was the perfect example. I knew he'd order the lobster, and I knew he'd get jealous of my Moscow Mule and want one for himself. But I didn't know that one of Jalen's friends would randomly deliver a homemade birthday cake that night, or that Jalen would be touched enough to cruise down Bourbon Street while lugging that unwieldy box. My biggest regret of my entire Jalen friendship was never snapping a picture—there was Jalen Rose moving through a swarm of mostly drunk people, all six feet eight and a half inches of him, holding a birthday cake box as people stared and shouted his name. It just seemed fitting and weird and funny and all so Jalen.

The man isn't even sneaky-famous; he's openly and undeniably famous. In the early 1990s, the Fab Five was just as well known as Arsenio, Tupac, Denzel, Snoop, and Dre. Something like forty million people watched C-Webb mistakenly call timeout in that Carolina game. Everyone who played basketball, at any level, started wearing baggier shorts and infusing extra swagger in their game because of Jalen and Jalen first. (And yeah, I include myself, a dorky white kid attending a mostly Irish-Catholic college in Massachusetts.) In 1998, Jalen's Pacers took Jordan's Bulls to the brink of a stunning Game 7 home defeat, the closest MJ came to blowing any of his six titles. In the 2000 finals, the Pacers gave Shaq and Kobe everything they could handle. You're talking about twelve to twenty million viewers per night for any of those games. It's one of many reasons why people always approach Jalen just to say they named their child after him—not just male babies, but female babies, too. I stopped noticing after a while. It's just part of being around him. People loved those teams, and those games, and especially, him. He was always the coolest member of the Fab Five, their heart and soul, their trendsetter, their chief trash-talker, their best interview, their fearless leader and crunch-time creator.

I never knew him in college, but like so many others, I felt like I did. He's been famous since he was eighteen years old, only he never went Macaulay Culkin on us. Fame suits him. He knows every famous black person between the ages of twenty-five and fifty-five—literally, all of them—but he'd never brag about it. He loves being around all types of people. When he moves in crowds with people yelping his name (JAAAAA-LENNNNNNNN!!!), he's learned to never stop moving. Puts in the time, makes people feel good . . . but never comes to an actual stop. If he stops, that's it. He'll get swarmed. Even on Bourbon Street—while wearing a suit and hauling a birthday cake. It made no sense at all, but it made total sense, because that's Jalen Rose.

We became friends because we love basketball, we love to work hard, we make each other laugh, we love early hip-hop, we love *Good Times,* we love our daughters, and we love Larry Bird. That's really it. In so many ways beyond the obvious ones, we're polar opposites. My dad is my best friend; Jalen never met his father. I'm a Celtics fan; he's a Pistons fan. I grew up in a Boston suburb and went to prep school in Connecticut; he had the flip side of that experience in every respect. Same for our college experiences. Same for our professional experiences—me writing about sports, him playing them—and then eventually, we crossed paths and became mismatched brothers for life. My favorite Jalen quality: his uncanny ability to slide into any social situation. It's truly remarkable, surpassed only by his generosity and steadfast determination to remain a role model for everyone back home. Everything he's done with his charter school in Detroit, the Jalen Rose Leadership Academy, will outlive him long after he's gone. And like everything else Jalen does, he's involved. Didn't just slap his name on the school and hand it over to people. He runs the thing.

When I found out Jalen was writing a book, I knew it would work because he's lived the most fascinating life, hands down, of anyone I ever met. (If you're keeping score, Jalen left out about 298 Jalen After Dark classics that would have sold more copies. It's really a shame. THE MAN STARRED IN THE NBA FOR THIRTEEN YEARS! AND WAS REALLY REALLY FAMOUS! For a married guy with two kids, there is nothing more exciting than Jalen saying the words "I shouldn't tell this story . . .") Over the past four decades, he crossed paths with hundreds of characters, overcame more adversity than anyone realizes, and somehow kept his trademark sense of humor the entire time. Jalen has no secrets; he's the most up-front person I know. Most ex–NBA stars avoid discussing life on the road, or the reasons behind petty feuds, or even the things most players really care about (like women, women, and also, women), but Jalen has been candid in his *Grantland* podcasts for four years and counting. He can't hide *anything*. It's just not in him. Most celebrities would be ashamed to discuss the days when they had bad acne or choppy teeth, or the ghastly Draft Day suit they never should have worn. Jalen brings that stuff up all the time. He's proud that he came from nothing. He wears every life scar like a badge of honor. He has a fear of conflict that's both hilarious and adorable; our buddy Jacoby and I tease him about it all the time. He tells his friends that he loves them, tells them that he's proud of them for no reason, hugs them just for the sake of hugging them. If he was your friend or your teammate, at any point in time, then he has your back for life.

I feel the same way about my own friends, actually. That's probably why we gravitated toward each other. One time we traveled to Austin to film a barbecue video for *Grantland.* We stayed at the St. Cecilia Hotel, only the most unexpectedly beautiful hotel in America. Jalen had a garden in the back of his room, as well as a flowered blue robe that he immediately threw on. He lounged on a swinging bench facing the garden, immediately falling sound asleep in his robe; naturally, I snapped multiple photos for blackmail material later. (He looked like a failed 1980s WWE character that was loosely based on Prince Akeem from *Coming to America.*) After Jalen woke up, we headed to a local bar to play shuffleboard and watch hockey. (Two things you wouldn't expect Jalen to do, right?) The locals kept approaching Jalen and grabbing their ninety seconds apiece before eventually leaving him alone. Since we were surrounded by Jacoby, a few other *Grantland*ers, and my two best friends from college, we might have ordered a beverage or two. Jalen was especially giddy because Fab Five teammate Ray Jackson was en route; once Ray waltzed through the door, it felt like watching Andy and Red reunite at the end of *College Hoops Shawshank*. And I was so happy to see my two college buddies again, and Jalen was so happy to be with his old college buddy again . . . and everything just kind of made sense. We had nothing in common and everything in common. For one night only, we had mutated into the new Fab Five. It's ridiculous, but that's how it felt. And it was because of Jalen Rose. The man has a knack for making everyone feel like he's been their friend forever. I bet you feel that way after you finish this book.

INTRODUCTION

I've always tricked out my cars, even when I didn't have enough money for gas. I'm from Detroit, the automobile capital of America, so I take pride in my rides. Back in high school, my friends used to call me Inspector Gadget because I messed with my cars so much. I once had a Dodge Omni that you had to start by turning the key, pressing the gas, and then hitting a switch by the clutch. It was like opening a trick door—no one could do it but me.

When I got to the NBA, I bought the biggest vehicles on the market, including a burgundy Chevy Suburban I called the Ice Box and, later, a Ford Excursion. I refashioned the Excursion's entire back half like a limousine, with a leather U-seat, a divider, and two TVs. It was unlike anything else on the road, which was exactly what I wanted.

But inside that Excursion, I came to a realization I'll never forget:

If you're driving alone at 2:00 a.m., wondering *What the hell am I going to do now?*, it doesn't matter what kind of car you're in.

You might have expected this book to start on a basketball court with the Fab Five at the Final Four. Or maybe at the NBA Finals, when I went up against Shaq and Kobe. But there's plenty of time to get to all of that. The best place to start is the day my life changed: Tuesday, February 19, 2002, driving north on I-65.

That night, the playoff-bound Pacers traded me, their leading scorer, to the Bulls, the absolute worst team in the NBA. The deal was preceded by shady leaks to the press and untruths (more on that later), but the only thing I said publicly at the time was "In every adverse situation, successful people find opportunity."

I was serious.

I could have taken a day or two to get myself together before I traveled to Chicago. Instead, I'd gotten on the road right away. A few days before, I had packed most of my stuff, knowing what was coming. When I got the call that the deal was done, I threw it all into my truck, got on the road, and drove north on I-65, straight to a hotel in downtown Chicago. The next morning, I woke up early, took my physical at 7:00, met with coach Bill Cartwright at 8:00, and got cleared to play. That night, without ever practicing with my new team, I scored thirty-six points to lead us to victory over the Knicks. Win number thirteen of the season. The Bulls won three straight games after my arrival before we spiraled back down into another stretch of losses. Which confirmed what I already knew driving to Chicago.

I was going to have to find something to keep me busy during the playoffs.

THREE OF the previous four years I'd played basketball through Memorial Day with the Pacers. We had gone to two Eastern Conference finals and one NBA Finals. In college, I'd been to two Final Fours with Michigan. In high school, I'd been on two state title-winning teams. But the Bulls weren't going anywhere after the regular season except home. And I knew I wasn't going to be ready to go home in April.

A few weeks into my time in the Windy City, I called a producer I'd met a few years earlier during a BET interview. She'd given me her card and told me to call her if I ever had any ideas. Now I did. The idea I pitched her was simple: to have their show *MAAD Sports* send me to the NBA Finals and let me report on the series. All she had to do was send the camera. I'd take care of credentials, access, and everything else. After a bit of selling, I got her to agree.

That was the start of my second career, begun while the first one was still going strong. I became a member of the media.

Now, more than a decade later, ESPN pays me good money to talk about basketball almost every day throughout the season. I dedicate a lot of time to my job, but like playing basketball, it doesn't feel like hard work because it's what I want to be doing. If you've listened to my podcast or follow me on Twitter, you know I have a mantra for what I try to do on my job:

Got to give the people what they want.

What do I mean? Be honest, unfiltered, unbiased. Raw, refreshing, real. Give people the kind of insight and understanding they don't get anywhere else. Be an alternative in a space that is too often preoccupied with people being politically correct. Explain why conventional wisdom often doesn't have a clue. And do it all without getting fired.

Millions of people follow sports every day, but too often they're reading contrived story lines that have nothing to do with the truth.

People want the real story, and that's what you'll get from me in this book. I'm here to share some tales and make you laugh, and also to be truthful and to make you think. I hope you learn from this book, but I also hope that you don't agree with everything I have to say. I want to start conversations, and even better, arguments.

I've faced a ton of adversity, and made a ton of mistakes. I've learned from all of it, and I've become a better man because of it. That said, if you told me I was going to end up here when I was driving to Chicago that night, I would have been a whole lot happier.

Because it was February, and the Bulls had twelve wins.

Twelve.

FIRST QUARTER

Growing Up

1. From a Freezing-Cold Night to a Dusty Film Room, or How I Discovered That I Was Meant to Be an NBA Player

You can still see the bump on my forehead.

It was January 30, 1973, the middle of the night in the middle of winter in Detroit—which means it was damn cold—and my mom started feeling things. She already had three kids, so she knew what those feelings meant. But unlike with those previous kids, she didn't have a husband to get her to the hospital. She'd gotten divorced, and the father of this new baby was nowhere to be found. So she called her brother, my Uncle Len, and told him she needed a ride to the hospital.

Two quick things about my Uncle Len that make him a good person to call in that situation: one, he is as cool as Marvin Gaye under pressure, even if you wake him up in the middle of the night; and, two, he has always had a lot of automobiles. Everyone's into cars in the Motor City—we care about our cars as much as we care about our houses. Len was a mechanic, and for this particular urgent voyage, he chose the 1970 Fiat, which could go for a month on six dollars of gas.

Len lived about ten minutes from us, but the hospital my mom wanted him to go to, Botsford General Hospital, was miles away, in the suburbs. There was a hospital in our neighborhood, but my mom was smart and knew the difference between city hospitals and suburban hospitals. Botsford General was going to be cleaner, with better doctors, better nurses—better everything. Still, there was a problem: I was coming out fast. The Fiat could weave through traffic pretty good, but Uncle Len didn't start actually running reds until after her water broke. When he pulled into the driveway, he was honking his horn nonstop for the emergency room staff to run out. They rushed over with a gurney, but it was just a little too late. When I came out, with my mom still halfway in the car, I basically fell out onto the street, on my head.

It sounds worse than it was, because the only souvenir I have from the adventure is that small bump on my forehead that never went away.

WE LIVED on the west side of Detroit. When I was real little, our house was a two-family home right off 6 Mile and Greenlawn. The room I shared with my brothers Bill and Kev was upstairs, down the hall from my mom, and my sister Tam lived downstairs with my grandmother. Tam was the princess, with her own room, decorated all in pink. Bill, Kev, and I were stuck in the slanted attic. They had the bunk bed; I got the mattress on the floor.

Bill and Kev are both ten years older than me, so when I was little, they were already off at school, doing their own thing. The task of watching me basically fell to whoever was home, which meant my mom and my grandma were like tag-team wrestlers, coming in and out. Mom worked days at Chrysler as a keypunch clerk, and Grammie worked the graveyard shift as a nurse. And the truth was, if they weren't working, they were often sleeping, because when else were they going to do it? So I was left to figure out things for myself, even when I was as young as five or six. That certainly wasn't my mom's or my grandma's fault. They were doing everything they could to make sure we had that roof over our heads.

We never struggled to the point where we didn't have a roof, but we sometimes had to eat popcorn for dinner or mayonnaise sandwiches for lunch. And sometimes we didn't have hot water for showers, or couldn't pay for our heat in the winter, so we had to sleep in hoodies and skullies and socks. And at one point, my mom had a car that had a hole in the floor—if you removed the mat, you could see the street going past. Looking back, it wasn't exactly pleasant. But at the time, as a young kid, how did I know any better? I still have a Thanksgiving card that I made in school for my family when I was young. I glued a family portrait to the paper, and in crayon I wrote, "From Jay. To My Pretty Family." And I meant it.

Furthermore, my mom wasn't the kind of person who complained about what we didn't have. She had far too much pride, and far too much confidence in herself that she would figure something out. When she could, she worked a second job as a waitress at a bar called the Chez Beau over on Livernois Avenue. When no one else could watch me, I'd have to go over there with her. I'd play pinball, drink some Shirley Temples, even try and help my mom by making jukebox runs. Customers drinking cocktails and smoking cigars would give me a coin to play the Spinners, the Four Tops, the Isley Brothers, whatever. It's how I first got into music, and it was a good way to hustle a few extra dollars in tips. The Chez Beau wasn't exactly a club in South Beach, but it was a popular place for a while, and at some point or other, it became clear to me that it was where my mom had met my dad.

I GUESS technically, Kev and Bill and Tam are my half siblings, but I've never thought of it that way. Even though I knew I had a different father than they did, it's not like their dad was ever really around much either. My mom's ex-husband is actually where we all got the name Rose. With no dads around, I think we all just became hardened by the situation. My brothers didn't talk about it, I didn't talk about it, and my mom made clear those men were not worth talking about. Honestly, I don't even think I ever asked her about my dad until middle school. Not one question.

I had plenty of adults in my life setting me straight anyway. My grandma is ninety-seven years old, and I'm still afraid of her. Grammie's philosophy has always been simple: You own the things that don't cost anything. You own your pride, your dignity, your self-esteem. Those things, no one can take away from you. She's the kind of neat freak who always covers her sofas in plastic, saves her food in the refrigerator in ziplock bags (once you open something—it goes in a bag), always makes sure there's a napkin under the glass on the coffee table. And growing up, you knew not to mess with that. With her working nights, she'd usually sleep during the day when I was at school and take me on errands with her in the afternoons.

I remember one time she went into a store and left me in her car, and I got thirsty. There was no water in the car, so I went into her purse and took a bunch of pieces of Clorets gum. When she came back, I freaked out, nervous she'd get mad at me with a mouth full of her gum. So I quickly rolled down the window and tossed it out. Well, a few minutes later I stuck my hand out the window, and I'll never forget the feeling of that gum, stuck on the side of the car, right where it left my hand. I tried to rub it off, peel it off, do whatever I could. We got home, I got out and took a look, and that gum was still all over the side of that car. I tried to stand there and block her view, but she was waiting for my help with the grocery bags, and about ten seconds later I got busted. She marched right past me into the house to her room to grab "the strap," which she always kept wrapped around the doorknob of her room. And with Grammie, the neat freak, it was always sort of a sloppy, wild whipping—anywhere she could get you: head, face, body. And you'd get it in the exact spot wherever the crime had taken place. So that time she just came back out and whipped me right there next to the car, and kids from the whole neighborhood could see me getting it as they were walking home from school. I remember my sister coming home and yelling, "Leave him alone, Grammie!" and me hollering like she was killing me. Because she was.

Bill and Kev were characters, too. We used to say Kev was like J.J. from *Good Times*, always finding things. He'd come home with these random stray dogs that would become pets for a few weeks or months. I remember we had a German shepherd named Champ, and a Doberman named Capone. I also distinctly remember the garage being stacked high with hubcaps and car emblems. Who knows where they came from. Bill was always more of the work-man, headed toward a nine-to-five lifestyle. I was eight or nine when they finished high school and Kev went off to the army and Bill went off to work, leaving just me and my sister in the house.

Fortunately, there was a big village around me to make sure I learned the rules of the world, and of the street. And at the time, the rules of the street were a lot more important.

JALEN WAS a name my mom came up with on her own. She liked the name Jason, but she wanted something more original. The *Ja* is for James, my dad, and the *len* is for my Uncle Len, who (almost) got me to the hospital when I was born. Twenty or so years later, my uncle was in a mall in Detroit and heard a mom yell after her kid: "Jalen!!!" He went up to her and asked how she came up with the name, since he'd never heard it anywhere else before. She said she'd heard it on that basketball player at Michigan and liked it.

I've always had a lot of pride about being named for Len. Len worked as a mechanic for Pontiac for decades, and he did well. Like I said, he always had at least a few cars, including a Corvette, a Bonneville, and that little Fiat, and he had a nice house on the west side a few neighborhoods over from us. He had two daughters, my cousins Traci and Tonya. We used to have Christmas at Uncle Len's, where there was a piano in the living room, and where I got my first glimpses of what being rich looked like.

Len and my mom were the two youngest children of Gram-mie and my grandfather, who everyone called Big Daddy. By the time I was old enough to know anything, Big Daddy and Grammie had gotten divorced, and he had moved back to his hometown of Bainbridge, Georgia. He'd worked at Ford for years but then moved south and opened a convenience store, Hicks Grocery, right next to his house. (His last name was Hicks.) Big Daddy was the first vision of cool I ever got: always immaculately dressed, with a peacoat and a hat. He called me Long Boy. "Hey, Long Boy," he'd say to me. "Don't smoke Kool. Be cool." Even though he'd moved away, Big Daddy would come up for a month or so every year, to make sure everyone was doing all right and give out some cash to those who needed it. And then in the summers we'd all get in a car and drive down to Georgia to spend a few weeks there, hang out, barbecue, all that good stuff. It was a long drive—we'd leave in the morning and get down there at night, though there was one time when we got lost and it took a full twenty-four hours. At the wheel that time was the man who was named for Big Daddy, his and Grammie's oldest son: the one and only Paramore Hicks Junior.

In Detroit, my Uncle Paramore is unquestionably the most famous member of my family, far more famous than me. When I'm in town, and I'm at a game, or a restaurant, or a store, people come up to me all the time and ask how my uncle's doing. He's battled some health problems over the last few years, but once you sit down and get him talking, you'll discover it hasn't slowed him down on the inside one bit.

Back in the day, people had no trouble spotting Uncle P. wherever he went—first off because of his car, which was always filled to the brim with what looked like all of his possessions. He looked like a man who'd just been kicked out of his house. But my Aunt

Barbara wasn't ever sending him anywhere—it was just the way Paramore liked to roll. And he rolled everywhere: to the community center, where he was always involved with kids; to the bowling alley, where he ran like four leagues at once; and to work at the Ford plant, where he was a leader in the union and was known across the company for his art skills.

Uncle P. wasn't strictly an industry guy, making his money in the factory. He was a hustler. Like his dad, Uncle P. has his own signature saying: "Have mind, will create." If you talk to him long enough, and there's a pen and paper around, he'll sketch a portrait of you in about ten minutes. Years ago, you'd also be able to find him downtown, drawing pictures of people's faces for a couple of extra dollars. In his working days, when someone famous, like Jesse Jackson, came to visit and give a speech at the factory, Paramore would do a sketch on a big Styrofoam board and proudly present the portrait to the subject in question. Retiring executives would get the same treatment.

At family parties, Uncle P. would break out one of the hundred magic tricks he knew, dazzling the kids, and a few adults, too. He'd shave his head in the summer, nice and clean, before a lot of people did that, and then charge kids "a nickel to touch, and a quarter to smooch." Then he'd use the money to take all of us to a baseball game or something. He was kind of like our family's version of Muhammad Ali: always entertaining, always the center of attention.

If it sounds like I look up to Paramore, it's because I do. Oh, and then there was the time he saved my life.

.   .   .

BACK IN the day, the pool in Paramore's backyard was where everyone in the neighborhood learned to swim. (The pool is now his botanical garden, filled with plants and trees.) Every summer, kids would come over for lessons taught by the pool owner himself. The only requirements were to bring your own towel, and a cup of bleach that he'd toss into the water as some sort of chlorine substitute. And if you weren't clean, which he'd determine by looking at the insides of your wrists, he'd get his hose and rag and rinse you off before you jumped in. The rest of your body could be full of dirt, but for some reason, your wrists had to be clean. He was happy to teach you, but you weren't getting into his pool with dirty wrists.

A few kids weren't into swimming at all. Maybe the water was too cold, maybe they didn't want to get wet, maybe they just didn't feel like it. I know all the excuses pretty well because they all applied to me. I was one of those kids you weren't getting in that pool if you tried. It wasn't a big deal until one winter when I was eight or nine and playing with my cousin Tia'von, Uncle P.'s daughter. It was a Saturday, Paramore's day off, and that meant he spent almost the whole day inside, in front of his crazy TV setup: four small monitors stacked on top of one another, broadcasting what he called "Hanger Vision." He didn't get regular cable, and instead used a collection of wire hangers to get a signal. On this Saturday he sat there in his shorts watching cartoons in Hanger Vision, occasionally dozing off and just catching up on his rest.

Outside, the pool had a gate around it to protect against kids walking on the ice that usually froze over on top of it before Paramore got a chance to put the cover on. That day, though, it was just too enticing, and Tia'von and I were inside the gate, playing a su-perhero game. I was Steve Austin, the old Six Million Dollar Man, and she was supposed to be the Bionic Woman. And for whatever reason, in character, I determined that jumping over the pool was something worth trying. Even if it was at least ten, maybe fifteen, feet across. I *was* the Six Million Dollar Man. Tia'von and I were going to do it together: I'd count to three, run back to the wall, bounce off it like it was a turnbuckle or something (I was already watching too much wrestling), and then we'd both jump. Today Tia'von is the principal of a school for special-needs kids, meaning she's pretty smart. She proved it that day. When we got to the edge of that pool, she stopped. I jumped.

My jump got me halfway over the pool before gravity won out and I dropped right through the ice, into the freezing pool water. Me, the kid who didn't feel like learning to swim.

Very quickly, two heroes sprang into action. First, Tia'von ran in-side to rouse my uncle, semiconsciously watching Elmer Fudd, and screamed at him to go to the backyard to do something. Also watch-ing the scene unfold was Uncle Paramore's dog, Wolf. Wolf ran onto the ice and got his teeth into the hood of my winter jacket, which wasn't exactly enough to keep me above water but did keep me near the hole long enough for Uncle P. to sprint outside in his boxer shorts and then promptly lose his balance on not just the ice, but on all the crap that Wolf had been depositing atop it all winter. So *boom*—down goes Uncle Paramore through the ice, hard. Under-neath the freezing-cold water, he looked around and found himself face-to-face with me, eyes and mouth wide open. He grabbed me, lifted me up, and then slipped again as he tried to climb out. But when my head hit his shoulders, I started coughing, and he knew I was going to be okay.

Right next to Tia'von, whose face was drenched in tears, Wolf the Dog was waiting for us on the side of the pool, wagging his tail, happy as could be.

I DON'T want you to think that men like Big Daddy, Uncle Len, and Uncle P. were perfect human beings, because that's not the point. They had a few beers at night, they smoked, they pissed off their wives occasionally. But more important, unlike so many other men on the west side of Detroit in the late '70s and '80s, they were there. They didn't disappear on their families, on their sons and daughters, on their responsibilities. And because of that, kids like me, and Tia'von, and my other cousins Traci and Tonya, and my brothers and sister, and my friends—we all learned things from them. How to live, and how to lead. And what success looked like. Maybe they weren't rich by everyone's standards, but they were bosses to us.

Then there was one more lesson I learned from those men. How to compete.

Because that television setup Uncle P. had in his room wasn't just for watching cartoons. The monitors were also all attached to different video game consoles. Intellivision. ColecoVision. Atari 2600. Video horse racing. Video baseball. He always had the latest model, and kids were always welcome to come inside and try their hand at beating the master. And Uncle P. didn't just beat you with his skills. He beat you with his head, and with his mouth. He would say whatever he had to say to get you out of your game, and before you had a chance to figure out how to respond, he'd won. It wasn't just about trash-talking, it was about being competitive.

And you couldn't just leave and go play outside after you lost. If you wanted another shot, you had to sit there, and wait until your turn came again. That built mental and emotional toughness. Waiting it out meant you couldn't look or be weak and fragile. I remember sitting for two hours to get another shot, stewing as I took more lip from Uncle P., and whoever else was in the room. Those were the rules, and those rules made you care about winning, not just in the video game battles, but in whatever other games we played outside.

Out there, when we played football in the street, or basketball, we talked trash just like Uncle Paramore did. Winning wasn't just about scoring more than the other guy—it was about making sure he knew you were scoring more, and that you were going to do it again, and again, and again. Not really to be mean, but—even if we didn't realize it at the time—to increase that edge you had on your opponent. It's probably how Uncle P. beat us for years after we were as good as him at Donkey Kong or Pac-Man or whatever it was. And it's why as the years would go on, that part of the game would remain a central piece of my repertoire.

Not to mention that when you told the guy what you were going to do, and then did it, it felt as good as anything in the world.

Still does.

TALKING TRASH as ten-year-olds was, admittedly, a pretty direct route to fighting. While things stayed civil in front of the video game console, thanks to Uncle Paramore's supervision, out on the court we'd lose control pretty often. The good thing was, these were the days when kids could just fight with their fists. There wasn't going to be some idiot who ran off and got his brother's gun or something stupid like that. I won some brawls, I lost some—but I was definitely in the middle of more than some.

We were all friends, but I was an easy target. Kids knew that I wet the bed until I was in the fourth grade—I tried to hide it by flipping the mattress all the time and washing my pajamas by myself, but there was nothing I could do when friends came over and my room smelled like piss. So I was Mr. Peebody, or Pee Boy, or whatever they came up with that day. I also got teased for being skinny, for having bumps on my face, for having horrible "rock teeth." (I got veneers when I got drafted by the Nuggets. It was the first trip to the dentist of my life.) In those fights, in those games, I learned about how to defend myself and how to stand up for myself.

Of course, I was also learning how to play the games. We played whatever was in season. In our version of basketball, we put milk crates on telephone poles to serve as hoops, meaning if you weren't careful driving to the "basket," you'd end up with a face full of wood. So that's how, in my earliest days, I started developing some three- or four-foot touch shots and flip shots in the lane. Sometimes when it was too cold or raining, my best friend, Mike Ham (short for Hamilton), and I would take hangers out of a closet in his house on Virginia Park Street, put two together with some tape to create a net, and then get some foil and put a sock around it for a ball. His grandmother hated when we did that, because the games could end with a broken lamp or two.

I wasn't supertall yet in those days, but I was tall enough, and from the start I was one of the better players in the neighborhood.

But other things got in the way of my game. Most of all, my behavior. I got into trouble so often as a kid that my mom kept moving me from school to school, trying to find one that fit. In fourth and fifth grades, I ended up living with my Aunt Jackie, my grandma's sister, at her house on the east side, at 6 Mile and Fleming, so I could go to a new school where I might behave better. Aunt Jackie was a teacher, and the school was near her house. Then, in sixth grade, I moved back home, and my mom sent me to St. Cecilia's, which was known not just for being a good school, but also as the basketball mecca of Detroit.

WITH ALL due respect to Mike Ilitch, the owner of the Detroit Red Wings, one of the most successful teams in all of sports over the last quarter century, Detroit is not Hockeytown. It's a hoops town. From streetball to high school hoops to college teams to the Pistons, basketball is the city's real number one sport. And for a long time, a man named Sam Washington at St. Cecilia's was at the center of the sport in town.

Sam was not only the head of athletics at the school, he also ran programs at all different levels of play, from Pro-Am leagues all the way down to youth teams. A former sports star back in the day, he started his reign in the late '60s, at the height of racial tensions in Detroit, as a way to do something for young people in the community. And he got things done by being a friend to everyone. For example, I once heard that in the early days of the program, he asked his friend Dave Bing, a star on the Pistons, to bring his team down to play at the gym, to bring more attention to what he was building. Then, not long after, when Bing was holding out for money in a new contract and getting fined five hundred dollars a day, he told his friend Sam he couldn't help him pay for a new gym floor. So Sam went to the Pistons, asked them what they were doing with the money they were collecting from Dave, and got his new floor a few months later.

As a kid, I knew Sam was the large man who'd sit by the door of the gym in his collared shirt and dress pants, working as athletic director and security chief all in one. Kids' parents would drop them off at the gym and not have to worry for a while because "Sam had them." And no matter what kind of kid you were, you wanted to play at St. Cecilia's because of everyone else who played there: George Gervin; Earvin "Magic" Johnson; and Magic's predecessor as the greatest point guard to ever come out of Michigan, Curtis "C.J." Jones.

Even before my mom sent me to the school, I was a "Ceciliaville" kid—that's what they called the day camp there. When camp was done for the day, I'd stay at the gym and hang around the court while older guys played in high school games or Pro-Am games. I watched guys with names basketball fans would recognize— Derrick Coleman, Steve Smith, Mark Macon, Doug Smith, among others. I'd get rebounds for them while they warmed up, make runs to the store down the block for food or a drink, anything I could do to get closer to the players. I loved being around the gym, and being around basketball.

But even for Sam Washington, it wasn't easy to get an eleven- or twelve-year-old fool like me to focus on really getting any better at the game.

.   .   .

I NEVER thought of myself as a bad kid, even if I did get into my fair share of trouble when I was little. I always did okay in school, though I was one of those kids who would finish my work real fast and then mess around in class. There were also plenty of fights, some of which got me suspended, and one of which ended with me breaking my finger on my adversary's head. That certainly wasn't good for my basketball prospects and was just one of many times I lost my spot on the team at St. Cecilia's. Most of the others, my mom took me off the team, usually when I got caught stealing, something that I got pretty good at. Not big-ticket items, but little things like candy bars, juice, baseball cards, and whatnot. If my mom found out about it, Sam would hear about it, too, because Sam heard about everything.

He would say, "I'm not calling you Jalen. I'm calling you Rose. You're going to have to earn it for me to call you by your first name." It was like I was a criminal and all that was missing was my inmate number. Not that I cared that much. Basketball was fun, but by this time, chasing girls and going to parties seemed even more fun.

Then one day, when I was in about sixth grade, old Sam Washington comes lumbering toward me after a practice, and he says, "Rose, I want to show you something. Let's go downstairs."

And I'm thinking, *We're going downstairs—this dude's about to kill me or something.* You didn't go downstairs to his office too often, and really only if you were in trouble. So we walk into this little room beneath the gym, and Sam pulls out one of those real old-school film projectors. The few other times I'd seen it, I had assumed it no longer worked. But there's Sam, blowing on it, dusting it off, and loading it with one of those big reels of film, all as I sit there watching, having no idea what he's doing. He finally gets it turned on, and up comes this black-and-white basketball footage of this one player. Jump shots, three-pointers, spin moves—this guy had it all. We sat there watching the clips for a few minutes, and then Sam spoke up.

"Do you know who this guy is?"

"No, sir," I replied.

"That's your father."

I looked over at him, snapping to attention.

"His name is Jimmy Walker. He used to play upstairs here when he played for the Pistons," he continued. "Made a few All-Star teams. Great college player, too."

I stayed silent, looking back and forth between the screen and Sam.

"If you stop fooling around and start taking this stuff seriously, you could go somewhere, Rose. But you're just wasting it now."

He turned off the projector, and we walked back upstairs. For the first time in my life, I knew who my father was. I can't say I was sad, I can't say I was happy, I can't even really say I was numb from the shock. Honestly, I was thinking just one thing.

I was going to the NBA.

2. How I Learned What It Really Takes to Become a Hustler

Every school I went to growing up in Detroit—elementary, middle, and high school—is now closed. You could have guessed that. You've read all the articles and seen the pictures of my city. You know about the hard times it's gone through, and how long the road to recovery is going to be, so it makes sense that the schools I went to twenty and thirty years ago wouldn't be there anymore.

But what you might not think about is what that means for the people still living in Detroit. Kids, in particular. Because if there aren't any good schools, everything dominoes from there. It's incredibly difficult for teachers to do their jobs in struggling schools, and almost impossible for kids to become quality students. And if you're not a quality student, there's almost no way to get into college, get a good job, and lead a decent life. If a kid living in Detroit today found out his father was an NBA player, and decided that he, too, was going to be an NBA player, I don't think he'd have even the slim shot I did of getting there. More important, if a kid today decided he wanted to be a doctor, or a lawyer, or a teacher, or start a business, he's not going to have much of a shot at those things without a thriving school. In my day, the odds were already low. Unfortunately, they're almost nonexistent now.

This is why I founded JRLA, the Jalen Rose Leadership Academy—a tuition-free public charter high school in the same 48235 zip code I grew up in. More on that later. But for the moment, this is what you need to know: If I were growing up now, not twenty or thirty years ago, I assure you things would have turned out differently for me. In today's climate, I probably wouldn't have gone to Michigan, I likely wouldn't have lasted more than a year in college, and I certainly wouldn't be a member of the Fab Five.

Fact is, I'm not even sure I'd make it through high school.

LIKE A lot of families on the west side of Detroit, we moved around when I was a kid. In second grade, we moved to a house on Rosa Parks Boulevard. Then, when I was twelve, we moved to a house on Puritan and Appoline that Uncle Len owned. That was where we were when my brothers started moving out on their own, giving me finally a room and walls I could decorate myself. I plastered one wall with *Sports Illustrated* covers full of athletes, another with *Source* or *Word Up!* covers full of rappers, and a third open wall with pictures of *Jet* beauties of the week. It made sense: the three things I was interested in as a teenager were sports, hip-hop, and girls. It just took a little while for the order of priorities to shake out the way it was supposed to.

Yes, my mindset may have changed that afternoon in the basement of St. Cecilia's with Sam Washington, but I can't claim to you that I dribbled a ball home that day or woke up the next morning at 6:00 a.m. to shoot baskets. I was a kid who liked to mess around, and that wasn't going to change overnight. I had already grown up way too quickly, thanks to my older brothers and the neighborhood I lived in. In grammar school, I remember thinking that the little feathers on a weed clip I found in my brothers' stuff were stylish. I actually walked around with a clip on my shirt one day, not knowing what it was. Too bad the teachers did. (I also loved the Rick James song "Mary Jane." Again, no idea what he was singing about.)

In class, I would throw paper airplanes and spitballs at my friends, anything to mess around. I'd pass notes to the girls, asking, "Do you like me?" with three boxes to check: "Yes," "No," or "Maybe." Hey, it was the quickest way to get an answer. I was also the one in the middle of all the trouble as we started to drink alcohol at eleven and twelve years old; started to smoke pot not long after that (and learn what a weed clip was); and started fooling around with girls (playing games like 7-11 and Hide and Go Get It). When some of my friends started stealing Cherokees, Topazes, Escorts, I'd go for the joyrides, put a towel over the ignition, drive around the hood, park it somewhere. It was a pretty normal life for a young kid in northwest Detroit.

Think of it this way: Imagine a kid today trying to avoid social media—Facebook, Twitter, texting. It'd be almost impossible. For us, drugs, violence, and crime engulfed us the same way. They were everywhere, and so was the desire to have things that were cool. Starter jackets. Cazal sunglasses. Levi's. Jingle Boots, Max Juliens, Nanny Goats. Fila suits. High-top Guccis. The list goes on. The hunger to be cool was endless. And I was walking a fine line—physically, mentally, and emotionally—between worlds. But it never got any worse for me. I never did any hard drugs or pills, never sold drugs, never committed any violent crimes, and never ended up in the YBIs— the Young Boys, Inc., an infamous Detroit gang led by Butch Jones.

The truth of why I didn't, like the truth of why any kid from the hood somehow avoids getting into anything worse, is complicated, and probably has a little to do with luck. Maybe the story that *usually* comes out in this kind of book is "I owe it all to my mom or my grandma or my uncle for steering me straight." But when were they going to have time to do that if, like I told you, they were working all the time?

As I look back, there were two main ingredients that pulled me through. First, I could see the criminals living the high life and making money off drugs, but I could also see the effects of that life. I watched people I knew transform from normal to crackheads. That was scary. There ain't nothing good about being a crackhead. Finding that out was a real reason not to smoke crack—a lot more convincing than "Just Say No." And in my era, that lifestyle in the hood was contained. If you didn't want any problems with drugs, if you weren't robbing, stealing, or killing, that crew left you alone. No one tried to force you in.

Second, of course, was basketball.

It took a few years from that day in Sam's office for my focus to tighten in on basketball exclusively. I played football, but I didn't like getting hit. (Just being honest.) I tried baseball for a while, too, but I didn't love it. Ironically, the most important reason my basketball game actually improved was thanks to a game you probably haven't heard of: Jaw Season. It was pretty simple: On the playground we'd look for kids whose mouths were open, tap them on the jaw, and see what happened. Well, a lot of fights happened, enough to eventually get me kicked out of St. Cecilia's after seventh grade.

That benefited my basketball game, because the next year I found myself at the school in my neighborhood, Precious Blood, where the team wasn't anywhere near as good as St. Cecilia's. But that meant if we had forty points in the game, I scored thirty.

Suddenly I wasn't just a little better than other kids when we shot half-dead balls at the basket pinned to a telephone pole in the street. These were real games, with real teams, and referees, and I dominated. And dominating was so fun it motivated me not to get kicked off the team every other week for being a knucklehead. Playing at Precious Blood gave me a taste of what it felt like to be a star, to feel different, to feel part of a special club.

Around that time, I also joined a local Amateur Athletic League team run by a coach named Curtis Hervey. I'd been invited to play on the team the previous year, but my mom wasn't going to drive me all the way to practice when I was acting out. That year I behaved well enough to convince her to take me to AAU.

But I still had to work a few other things out.

. . .

LEARNING HOW to compete is a huge part of becoming a good basketball player. The AAU team Curtis Hervey called "the Super-friends" was great before I got there. My first season we had strong players and won almost every game on our schedule. I didn't play too much. The turning point came at one of our championship games, in Saginaw, which is a hundred miles north of Detroit.

My brother Kevin had just come home from the army a few days before the game, so he was able to drive me up to Saginaw and watch me play. We won, but I played maybe like five minutes, total. A few in the second quarter, a few more in mop-up duty. Still, I was celebrating with the team on the court after our victory, as happy as everyone else, because this win meant we got to go to nationals. Afterwards, I went over to my brother, expecting congratulations. Instead, he cussed me out.

"Man, don't ever have me drive all the way up here to watch you sit on your ass! It's good that you won, but you did nothing!!"

It was the opposite of what you're supposed to teach kids in basketball—to support the team, cheer on your teammates, accept your role. But it also showed why a lot of traditional sports advice is wrong. No one content riding the pine and giving the best high fives is going to improve. If my basketball career was going to go anywhere, I needed to hear that message. It was one thing to walk around knowing my father was a pro and believing that was my destiny. It was another to put in the work to make it.

That summer I started playing every single day and working hard in a new way. Playing in every pickup I could at the park and the YMCA—all day, every day. The AAU game my brother watched was in June, and August was the national tournament. In those two months, I went from sitting the bench to getting real minutes to making the All-American team when we went to St. Louis for the tournament.

Now I was ready for high school basketball in Detroit.

WHEN I was growing up and going into my teenage years, the Pistons were on the rise thanks to Isiah Thomas and the Bad Boys, and Michigan was one of the top-ranked teams in the country. But the heart of hoops in Detroit then, and for generations before that, was high school basketball. The stars in the city were local celebrities to us, hailing from high schools like Cooley, Southwestern, Mackenzie, Pershing, and River Rouge. I mentioned Derrick Coleman and Steve Smith. Plus B.J. Armstrong, and going back further, George Gervin, who played at Martin Luther King. Even guys from places nearby in Michigan, like Glen Rice and, of course, Magic Johnson, were huge stars to us. That's the history we heard about on the playgrounds, at St. Cecilia's, and at practice with the Superfriends. We wanted to become a part of it.

Back then, the city had an open-enrollment system, which meant you could go to any school in the city as long as you were willing to ride the bus to get there for the bell. If you were an athlete, you tried to go to the schools with the best teams, the best coaches, and the best resources. For me, the decision on where to go was never a question. I knew exactly where I wanted to go.

High school teams used to sell out the gym at places like the University of Detroit and the Michigan State Fairgrounds Coliseum. And in eighth grade, I went to a game at the fairgrounds and watched a team play that mesmerized me. I remember all these people in the crowd wearing these clean white hats, with the team's logo in cursive on the front. "Southwestern," the hats read. And the star player nobody could take their eyes off was Anderson Hunt. You simply could not take the ball up on him. He'd get down into his defensive stance, and it was like trying to get the ball past a tiger or something. I'll never forget watching him in a sequence just before halftime. He drained two threes back-to-back, and then, as the clock ticked down and the point guard from the other team was bringing it up, Hunt stole the ball, went straight to the hoop, dunked it at the buzzer, and ran straight into the locker room without breaking stride.

Anderson Hunt was headed off to UNLV to win a national title with Jerry Tarkanian. But all I cared about was figuring out a way to go to Southwestern High School and play for the coach there, the legendary Perry Watson.

NO MATTER what else I tell you, one thing you can't forget about Perry Watson is that he was a child of the '60s in Detroit. He was a member of the class of 1968 at Southwestern High, which puts him at the epicenter of the Civil Rights movement and the racial tensions that surrounded it. Martin Luther King Jr. was assassinated two months before Perry graduated. The year before, as a high school junior, he lived through the 12th Street riot, when forty-three people died, more than a thousand were injured, and more than two thousand buildings were destroyed.

Before all that, Detroit's neighborhoods were stable. Perry's parents were just like my family, and like so many other black folks in Detroit: Everyone worked in the factory, and a lot of them became first-time home owners. Detroit represented the American dream to them. In the '60s, Detroit had the highest rate of home ownership among blacks in the country. They took pride in their neighborhoods and in supporting the young people there. Perry benefited from that upbringing, was a basketball star at Southwestern, and went to college, getting his teaching degree as well as a master's degree in guidance counseling. Then he went right back where he started: to work as a teacher, first in a local elementary school, and eventually, in 1979, as the basketball coach at Southwestern.

Through the '80s, Coach Watson built Southwestern into one of the city's best programs and one of the best programs in the entire country. The ingredients were simple: the best players wanted to play for him because they knew he was going to make them as great as their potential allowed. Then, from there, like any successful program, it was a cycle: winning bred more winning. More and more kids like me in Detroit wanted to join up, like a club. Coach Watson's club was a whole lot cooler than hotwiring cars, or smoking crack, or getting into whatever trouble was waiting for you on the street. The program was hard to get into, and it was not much easier to maintain membership.

At Southwestern, you couldn't just show up and join the team; you had to first play junior varsity. In addition, Coach Watson wasn't just running the varsity, he doubled as every player's guidance counselor. That was how he kept an eye on you in class, to make sure you weren't messing around. Even though we were just teenagers, we all bought in, because we wanted to play for the team, and we wanted to win. It's not much different in the NBA, to be quite honest. On bad teams, guys don't buy in. But trade a player to

San Antonio, suddenly he's a different guy in practice, in games, in everything.

When I came in as a freshman, Coach Watson's teams had been great, but not the best. The details are still painful to recount. They'd lost seven straight state championship games. Seven straight to stars like Glen Rice, Andre Rison, and Jeff Grayer. They were like Jerry West's Lakers teams in the 1960s. The losses gave every new player who came in a goal: to be part of the team that won the first state title. There was another stat, too, that drew us in (and impressed our parents): In his twelve years as coach, 96 percent of Coach Watson's players went to college. And not just the national recruits, the All-Americans, and the All-State players, but the reserves, too. Perry used his connections to get guys scholarships to have at least a shot at an education, and a different kind of future than they would have if they stayed in the city.

Why'd he do it? Why'd he care so much? Because as a child of 1960s Detroit, he'd been taught to care about the neighborhood, help nurture the community, and most of all, make a difference.

My education at Southwestern started the summer before freshman year. To play basketball in the program, you had to run cross-country in the fall and, even before that, prove you were in shape by participating in a forty-day boot camp workout supervised by Tony Jones, the JV coach. Conditioning was key if you were going to play at Southwestern, since Coach Watson ran a run-and-jump press that was akin to Nolan Richardson's "40 Minutes of Hell" at Arkansas and the "amoeba defense" at UNLV. Before that boot camp prior to my freshman year, all my conditioning work had been, to put it mildly, improvised. I used to wake up on Saturdays, watch cartoons, and alternate doing push-ups and sit-ups during the commercials. And then there was the time my buddy Mike Ham and I ran the three miles from his house on Virginia Park all the way to St. Cecilia's—with ankle weights on. Our thought was that when we took the ankle weights off, we'd feel lighter and be able to jump through the gym. It didn't work; it just made our feet sore.

The Southwestern camp, by contrast, was actually run similar to the way a lot of European clubs train today, with all of the players doing the same skills—centers working on crossover dribbles, power forwards practicing jump shots. Another freshman, Voshon Lenard, and a sophomore, Howard Eisley, were right next to me, all of us working on different skills than we were used to.

One of my biggest issues at that time was jumping off my left foot to make a right-handed layup. (Remember, I'm a lefty.) I worked on it for a week, and then one day, finally, just as I got it, we went outside for a break to get some air. I remember that day because it was right when KFC had come out with Chicken Littles, those little chicken burgers you could eat twenty of at a time. And outside was a guy who I'd never met, but who I liked instantly because in the open trunk of his car there were at least ten boxes of Chicken Littles. He'd brought them for all the players to chow down on during their break.

The guy's name was Ed Martin.

IN A place like northwest Detroit, it took a village. A lot of people looking out for a lot of other people, a lot of people working in the gray areas and the margins of the system to make sure everyone could pay their rent, pay their heating bills, their car bills, or anything else they might have needed. Ed Martin was one of those helpers. Like almost everyone else, he started out working in a factory, but then got injured on the job, which forced him to go on disability. So he got involved in a few other things, including a little bit of gambling (nothing unfamiliar in Detroit) and a little bit of loaning money to people who needed it. And then there was another thing that made Ed a lot like plenty of other people we all knew: He was a big high school basketball fan.

Ed had a big smile and an infectious personality and knew a lot of people, including Perry Watson. And like me, Ed was a big Southwestern fan. Hence he showed up that day—and lots of others—to bring us some Chicken Littles, or doughnuts, or whatever. I remember the first time I had seafood pizza—pizza with crab on it—was from a pie Ed Martin brought us from Pizza Papalis after an AAU game. Ed did other things, too—for young players all across the city, playing for all different schools and programs. If a kid was playing on old, torn sneakers and couldn't afford new ones, Ed would buy him a new pair at the old Blackburn Sporting Goods on Michigan Avenue. If he heard a mom had lost her job and he saw her son without a winter coat in January, he'd buy the kid a coat from Burlington Coat Factory. That kind of thing. Ed had some money in his pocket, and he wanted to spread it around the neighborhood. Basketball was how he got to know the kids, and basketball players were young people who had shots of getting college scholarships and doing great things with their lives. It made sense to invest in the future of the city.

We called Ed the Godfather—me, everyone on Southwestern, and plenty of others, including a tall kid who had joined the Superfriends named Chris Webber. I actually remember the first time Chris came in the gym. He had on this crazy outfit with all these layers, because it was freezing cold in the middle of winter in Detroit, and that's what you did to stay warm. But once all those sweats came off, and this gangly dude was in his short shorts, it was pretty clear how good he was. I think Chris was born at more than ten pounds and was always supertall for his age, but he was also superathletic. By eighth grade, every coach in the city was salivating for the chance to have him on their team. His mom had other ideas, deciding Chris would go to a private school, Detroit Country Day. It was in a whole different world from ours and would give Chris an entirely different high school experience than any of the rest of us had. We still played together in AAU ball on the Superfriends, though, and that included a lot of long rides to travel tournaments with Better Made chips, Faygo Pop, Run-DMC tapes playing on the bus. And a lot of nights in motels drinking Olde English and Wild Irish Rose and Mad Dog 20/20. We had our fun, and through it all, Chris and I became better and better friends.

WHEN I was young, I never focused on what we didn't have, because I didn't know what else was out there. If we didn't have heat, well, down the block they've got ten foreclosure notices posted on the front door. Though one of the things unique about my block on Appoline Street in particular was how stable it was. The Holmes family was across the street. My friend Trent lived there. His grandfather, Mr. Holmes, had lost his leg in the armed forces, but he still went to work every day and was another guy to look up to and talk to once in a while on the porch. The Robinsons were next door to them. Willie "Vedo" Robinson and I were the Dream Team whenever we played ball on the virtual full court we'd set

up on the street with two hoops. Both those families, plus the Eu-
bankses, the Greens, the Warrens—they all still live on the block
today. They're good people who created what seemed to me like
our own little nongated gated community.

Still, as I got older, I started learning a little bit more about how
the world worked, with regards to rich people and poor people
and the reality that what was available to some wasn't available to
others. Eventually, once you overhear your folks talking enough,
you figure out that the reason it took ten years for Uncle Len to get a
mechanic's job at the actual Pontiac plant, rather than a dealership,
was because they weren't looking to hire any black mechanics. And
the reason Uncle Paramore never had a prayer at getting a job in the
art department at Ford, rather than the part of the factory where
they worked with raw coke fuel, was because black people weren't
hired to work in the art department at Ford. When the things in
front of you in life reveal how messed up the system is, you lose
faith in the system pretty quickly. As a young kid, that could mean
getting into a lot of fights. As you get older, it's more about how you
think. You don't trust what people say just because they sound like
they know what they're talking about. You develop a contrarian attitude. Your instinct is to disagree with the status quo, and then, if
you can, to try and shake it up.

This informed who I grew into as a young man and as a basketball player. I was the kind of leader who wasn't going to stay quiet
in the locker room. I had learned early that if you don't say what's
on your mind to improve a situation, you're a fool. Part of the reason
I was always competitive was, everywhere I looked, I saw things
that I didn't have. Things I wanted.

Figuring out how to channel that competitiveness the right way was a long process. For example, when the Superfriends went to nationals in St. Louis, we came up against a team from Reston, Virginia, which included a player named Grant Hill. This team had new shoes, nice uniforms and bags; they had fans in the crowd who had had the means to travel to the tournament with the kids, and they had these cheesy organized cheers—stuff that was totally foreign to us. I pegged them as phonies and told all my teammates how this was going to be the easiest game all year. Well, we got on the court, and couldn't get the ball past the midline. They were much more organized, much more disciplined, and we got crushed by twenty-five points. Maybe those guys had more than us, but it didn't mean they couldn't play ball.

Losses like that taught me how to value winning, whoever the opponent. I eventually hung three jerseys in my locker at Michigan. Lawrence Taylor and Deion Sanders embodied the kind of rebels that I embraced, but Magic Johnson out of East Lansing, Michigan, was my ultimate favorite. Because of where he was from, yes. Because he was a tall point guard like me, yes. But more than anything, because he was all about winning. (Okay, that twenty-five-year $25 million contract he signed after his rookie season didn't hurt either.)

Playing for Southwestern we were, for whatever reason, to certain people in the city, the villains. High school basketball got a lot of coverage in the local paper, the *Detroit Free Press*, and one of the main writers about high school hoops was a guy named Mick McCabe. He's actually still there today—probably looking for ways to bash Southwestern High even though the school closed down.

(This chapter will give you the opportunity. You're welcome, Mick.) McCabe didn't like Perry Watson. According to Perry, it was a conflict that went back years, and had to do with McCabe trying to influence where Antoine "The Judge" Joubert, who played at Southwestern and was Michigan's Mr. Basketball in 1983, went to college. (The Judge ended up going to Michigan and winning two Big Ten titles.) McCabe used to write negative things about us all the time, and once I got big enough, he wrote negative things about me, too—before he even ever met me.

The team McCabe embraced was our archrival, Cooley, coached by Ben Kelso, featuring a Michigan Mr. Basketball in Mike Talley and a six-foot-eight, 280-pound brick of a young man with hops named Daniel Lyton. My sophomore year, my first on varsity, we beat Cooley in the PSL championship at Cobo Hall, and then they beat us in the state championship. The rivalry continued from there. The games we played against them every year are still, to this day, as intense as any games I've ever played. They didn't play music during games back then, so the chants from the fans were huge. I'll never stop hearing them in my head: "C-O-O-L-E-Y—Cool-AY, Cool-ay, Cool-ay High!" for them; and, for us, "South West, South South West," a takeoff on the song "South Bronx" by Boogie Down Productions. One time, when I was a junior, in a game against Cooley on our home floor, I went up for a dunk and got clotheslined by a player named Ken Conley, slammed to the ground, head first. Ask anyone who was there—I literally started convulsing on the floor. They had to put a stick in my mouth to make sure I didn't swallow my tongue. I was unconscious all the way until they wheeled me to the ambulance outside, the cold air waking me up. I woke up with my mom right there, crying because she was so nervous, looking at her son in a neck brace, people thinking I might be paralyzed and never play again.

I missed one game, against Chadsey High. Must be my hard head or something.

Still, that's not why I tell you the story. The game, and the injury, were big news, and there was an article in the paper about it, with my picture and my name splashed all across it. A few days later, my mom got a call from a woman asking if she could talk to me.

It was Jimmy Walker's ex-wife.

3. From Sitting at a Bar to the Sneaker Wars of the Twenty-first Century

To the people around me it was never a secret who my father was. Everyone in my family knew, and a lot of folks in the basketball scene in Detroit knew long before Sam Washington decided he'd tell me.

Nineteen seventy-two, when Jimmy Walker met my mom, was his last season with the Pistons. The team had drafted him as the top overall pick in 1967, after he'd led the country in scoring as a senior at Providence College. (That was actually the first draft after the NBA got rid of the territorial draft rights. If things had stayed the way they were for years before, then the Celtics probably would have grabbed Jimmy, and he never would have played for Detroit.) The bar where they met, the Chez Beau, was owned by a former Piston, Joe Strawder, which meant a lot of pros hung out there. It was no coincidence that my mom worked there for her second job. She's a huge basketball fan. Huge. To this day, if I call her on any given night, she's likely to be flipping around between games with the league package.

By the '72 season, Jimmy had fallen off somewhat from his college career but still made two All-Star teams for the Pistons. In

August of that year, he was traded to the Rockets, which meant he wasn't around when I was born the following January. He did, however, have other family back in Detroit and came back through once in a while when the Rockets played the Pistons. One time in 1973 or '74, when he happened to be in town and came by the Chez Beau, my Uncle Paramore was sitting at the bar. And Uncle P., as you might guess, went right up to Walker and asked him when he was going to come around and see his boy. The answer—"I'm going to"—was far too noncommittal for Paramore. He got in his car, drove to my mom's house, picked me up, and brought me right back to the Chez Beau. I was just a baby, so I fit right on top of the bar, right next to Walker. "That's your little man," Uncle P. said. "You should go and hook up with him." He wasn't too interested, so my uncle took me home a little while after that.

ONCE I found out who my father was years later I didn't bother my mom with it. I definitely didn't come straight home when Sam told me and ask her about it. Or, for that matter, my brothers or sister. I had grown up fast, and I was savvy enough to know that the topic wasn't a place to go with my mom. She was working hard to support us all on her own, and hammering her with questions seemed like another burden.

By the way, the wind blew in both directions. My mom would never bring a man home to the house. Sure, I met a few boyfriends over the years—there was one guy who owned the All-Seasons Party Shop, another who I remember drove a Lincoln—but they were never in the house at night or hanging around our family. She was totally focused on us, making sure we had what we needed.

Outside of our home was a different story. It was pretty cool to be able to say my father was an NBA player, particularly on the street when someone wasn't going to let me in their game. Like a show-off, I'd brag about being the son of Jimmy Walker, and, sometimes, that would get me in.

More privately, I was a huge card collector. Baseball cards, football cards, basketball cards, you name it. And at some point I ended up with a Jimmy Walker card, and for a long time I carried it in my pocket rather than leave it in the shoeboxes with the rest of the cards back in my room. On occasion, I'd have the card when bigger kids wouldn't let me into a game on a playground, and flashing it was another way to get me into the game. It was my driver's license, my basketball ID. And it worked.

But I never mentioned any of this to my mom.

By the time I got to high school, I had my own subtle ways of reminding myself who I was. Jimmy Walker wore number 24. So I wore 42. Little things like that, things other people might not have noticed, meant something to me. I decided that someday he'd know my name. I came close after that Cooley game in high school when his ex-wife called my house looking for me. (She actually first called Coach Watson, who asked my mom if it was okay to call.) She was very nice and sweet, and wanted to meet me. My mom said, "You should do it." So she ended up picking me up at my house with her daughter, and taking me shopping. She bought me a dress shirt and some dress clothes. For some reason, that was what she wanted to do. It was a nice day, and I thanked her, but after that day I never reached out again.

By that point, I was pretty busy anyway. I had to figure out where to go to college.

. . .

Please remember this fact—yes, fact—as you read this chapter: It is all about the money. It always is, and always has been. They may call it amateur athletics, but college sports is a for-profit enterprise. There are billions of dollars to be had, and if you run college sports at a school, getting as much of that pie as you can is your job.

Please also understand this opinion as you read this chapter: If college sports are all about the money, what's wrong with that? Money isn't a bad thing; money's a great thing. Money's what pays for heating bills and mortgages. Money's what pays teachers. Money's what you give poor people when you want to make them not poor anymore. Money's what rich people use to enjoy wonderful things. Money gets a bad rap in sports, where, for some reason, we try and pretend the whole enterprise is purely "for the love of the game," when it absolutely isn't. And thank God for that, because it wouldn't be nearly as interesting if it was.

Look, a man like Ed Martin, who helped out poor players in Detroit, was all about the money, because everything Ed Martin did for us was based on the reality that he had money and we didn't. That doesn't necessarily mean Ed was looking to profit from the kids he bought shoes and seafood pizza for, or, worse, to try and screw us in some way. Not a chance. Ed was one of us, and he wanted us to have what he had. I'm not saying that the man wasn't a hustler—everyone in the hood is a hustler. But in the hood, or, as we refer to it, on the block, hustlers can do a lot of good. That is what I was taught, closely coupled with another lesson: be careful about trusting people who come from outside the hood and tell you they have your best interests at heart.

That concept was never made clearer than by one of the most important things Coach Perry Watson did for us during the college recruiting process: He intercepted all the letters that came in from schools as early as our freshman year and kept them in a box until the end of our junior year. If you got a lot of letters, you just got a bigger box—but none of us ever got to see a single one. Today, kids start getting letters in junior high, if not earlier. Don't you think that goes straight to a young player's head? Makes them think they're better than they are, or that they don't have to work to reach their potential? All Perry wanted us to focus on was basketball, and so even though we knew there were college scouts and coaches in the stands at our games, we had a shield over us, protecting us from the reality that awaited us senior year, when it would come time to figure out what the next step would be.

Today, I don't think Perry, or any high school coach, would have any chance of pulling that on his kids.

Everyone else—the parents, the AAU coaches, the street agents—would find a way to band together and get him fired as revenge for keeping them from sniffing the sweet scent of money.

AS I write this, Perry Watson is about to turn sixty-five years old. Coach K, Gregg Popovich, and Pete Carroll are all around the same age or a little older than Perry. But he hasn't coached in more than five years, and whenever anyone asks him about it, he just shakes his head. It's not worth it, he says. The system's changed too much. The way he ran his program, looking out for his kids, would be impossible now. So the greatest coach in Detroit high school history (and maybe Detroit basketball history, when you consider what he did after Southwestern) is enjoying the retired life from standing on the sideline barking orders—he is now a scout for the Orlando Magic. He keeps in touch with his old players, and keeps tabs on their parents and their kids. I don't think he could look at me with a straight face and say he doesn't miss it. Problem is, the game he misses is gone.

My mom knew all about Perry Watson when she sent me to Southwestern. She knew she'd struck gold when I told her I was willing to catch two buses early in the morning to go from our house to school, to play for a man who was going to look after me, and straighten me out. Today, there are fewer and fewer parents who would feel that way. Nowadays, with the Internet and social media, there are scouting reports on ten-year-olds like LeBron James Jr. And everything's national. It wouldn't be a little local open secret that I was Jimmy Walker's son. It would be a national story on ESPN by the time I was twelve. Which would mean there would be a whole lot of people who would have come out of the woodwork to try and grab a seat on my train. Too many people for Perry Watson, or my mom, to keep away from me.

All that makes young talented players a lot different today. They, and the people around them, aren't going to be up for playing JV ball. The competition for touches, stats, and highlights among players headed into big-time recruiting is more intense and starts earlier than ever. And a program like Southwestern can't exist anymore.

WE LOST four games in my four years at Southwestern. I'm as proud of what we accomplished there as I am of anything else in my career, including Michigan. In retrospect, there could have been no more perfect place to play for a kid from the city. Playing at Southwestern made me love the game more than I ever had before. Even outside the team, I'd play pickup ball anywhere I could during those years: at the Northwest Activities Center, the Police Athletic League, and the Joseph Walker Williams Community Center. Meanwhile, at Southwestern, we worked harder than any other team, whether it was running 5-1-5-1-5s on sunny days (five laps around the track, a lap around the baseball field, and back again and again) or running the school hallways on rainy days. There was a tremendous level of discipline and professionalism expected of the team. On those rare occasions we lost, nothing was said on the bus ride home, and we definitely practiced that night when we got back.

Above everything else, though, winning was the most important part of my experience at Southwestern. Those early victories turned me on to winning, got me *addicted* to winning. I learned what it takes to win, and that is the most important ingredient in becoming a great player. Winners put winning first, which means they'll work harder at their games in practice (to win), and they'll do whatever's most important for the team (to win), from playing better defense to diving on the floor in pursuit of a loose ball to becoming a better teammate. That doesn't mean a winner will be happy to sit on the bench while his team wins, as I did at the start of my AAU days in middle school. Winners want to be part of the winning; they *need* to be part of the winning.

By high school, that's the kind of attitude I had. Failure was not an option. And with Voshon Lenard and Howard Eisley on my team—two of the best players in the state of Michigan, two future college stars (at the University of Minnesota and Boston College, respectively), and two future NBA veterans—I learned how to be a star playing next to other stars, catching lobs, dunking, hitting threes, playing suffocating defense. Together, we set out to win Southwestern a state title, beating everyone in our path, including our archrivals at Cooley, along the way. We did just that. In the title game my junior year, with our big man Elton Carter hurt, I jumped center. The night before the game, I remember visualizing Magic Johnson in the 1980 NBA Finals against the Sixers—fantasizing about how I could be like him. And then I did it, and we won. Winning that title was as sweet as anything I've ever experienced in basketball. After everything Coach Watson had done for us, we were able to deliver him the one thing he didn't have: the state title.

Then we won it again my senior year. We were named the best high school team in the entire country by *USA Today*. One other achievement of our dominant Southwestern team: Michigan's own Derek Jeter once said that after he played us with his high school basketball team, he realized it was time to focus on baseball.

Now, even though Coach Watson kept my letters in that box, I thought about where I was going to go to college all the time. From the start, just four schools appealed to me. First and foremost, UNLV. They were the best team in the country, and, looking back, their image certainly fit their team name, the Runnin' Rebels, and that was an image I naturally gravitated toward. Soon after the Palace of Auburn Hills was open, UNLV came to play a game there against Michigan State. The day before their game, the entire team came to a Southwestern game and made me like the school even more.

Then there was Syracuse, where Detroit's own Derrick Coleman had just gone to the Final Four. Another local connection there was Dave Bing, the Pistons Hall of Famer who added to his fame in Detroit by becoming a steel magnate after his playing days. Dave knew my family well, and he'd known Jimmy Walker when they were teammates. I worked at his company, Bing Steel, one summer in high school—one of the longest, hardest summers of my life. Nobody cut the basketball star any slack at all over there.

Dave was never that interested in talking to me about basketball, really. He was more about talking to me about life. He was giving back to Detroit, staying loyal and contributing. That concept factored into my two other top schools, Michigan State and Michigan. Staying close to home, close to my mom, who had supported me as

I'd become a star, and my grandma, who'd been making my scrap-
books going back to sixth grade at St. Cecilia's, was something that
made a lot of sense to me.

There was one other factor: I wasn't the only top recruit in the
city thinking about staying local.

THERE WERE plenty of reasons why Chris Webber and I shouldn't
have been good friends. First, while the rest of us were taking two
public buses across town to school at the crack of dawn, he was
going to a beautiful private school outside of the city, with big,
beautiful grassy fields; a parking lot filled with fancy cars; class-
rooms with rich kids; and the best education money could buy. He
straddled two worlds, and some people left behind on the concrete
resented him for that. I never saw it that way, though. To me, his
scholarship was an opportunity that his family wanted to take
advantage of, and I always had respect for that decision.

Another reason we weren't supposed to get along had to do with
basketball. Going back to our earliest days playing together on the
Superfriends, Chris was viewed as the prodigy who was definitely
headed to the NBA. True, I got lots of attention, especially at Southwestern, and, like him, I was a McDonald's All-American, a Dapper
Dan All-American, went to all the camps, and played against all the
other top players in the country. But there was only one Chris Webber. Local news cameras were following him around at practice,
treating him like a celebrity. Even Ed Martin started going to more
Country Day games than Southwestern games. (I remember Coach
Watson getting on Ed for that in a joking way.) Senior year, when it
was a foregone conclusion that Chris was going to be named Michi-

gan's Mr. Basketball, the top player in the state, I went to Coach and said, "Actually, I'm going to be Mr. Basketball. I'm gonna beat out Chris." That was my goal for the year, and I did everything I could to make it happen. I was the best player on my second state championship team that was again named the top team in the country. But Chris was still Michigan's Mr. Basketball.

And I was happy for him.

Part of my education was learning what competition is, and what it doesn't have to be. Playing on the same AAU teams for years and carpooling to games, being familiar faces for one another at all these national camps, the experiences Chris and I had together had made us good friends. So why did competing have to get in the way of that? Why couldn't my friend be my rival? Shouldn't it have been a good thing that I had someone to motivate me to go to the gym every morning, to get better every time I got out on the court?

From the start, I was never one of those guys who took my basketball emotions and turned them into my overall emotions. Sure, no one talked more than me on the court, and I got in my fair share of arguments and fights in games. But it never carried over anywhere else. Maybe that was because so many guys I played were coming from the same place as me. Maybe that was because at Southwestern, and on the Superfriends, I was used to playing with other great players and measuring myself against them even as I shared the ball with them. I was always able to be friends with my rivals off the court.

Being ranked behind Chris Webber didn't make me hate him; if anything, it strengthened our friendship. When we played together in AAU ball, I think Chris liked my style: my loud way of taking control on the court, my streetball Teflon Don mentality that provided a nice contrast from the private school league he easily dominated. We stayed close as senior year approached. And we both remembered the conversation we'd had back in eighth grade, when he told me that he was going to Country Day and not Southwestern.

"Let's not worry about high school," we said. "We'll go to college together instead."

THERE ARE a lot of people who deserve credit for creating the Fab Five, one of the greatest recruiting classes for any school ever. I think the guy who sometimes gets forgotten is Juwan Howard.

It's well known that Juwan was the first member of the Fab Five to commit to Michigan, and that was thanks to a long recruiting effort by Steve Fisher, Michigan's head coach, and Brian Dutcher, his top assistant, both now at San Diego State. Basically, for Juwan, there was one person more important than anyone in his life—his grandmother. She was the equivalent of my mom, my grandma, my uncles, Sam Washington, and Perry Watson all rolled into one. After a high school career that made him the best player in Chicago, on the day that Juwan announced he was going to the University of Michigan, his grandma died of a heart attack. A few days later, Coach Fisher and Coach Dutcher, sure enough, showed up at her funeral. If Juwan needed a sign of where the best place to go was, that was it. He knew he'd made the right decision.

Juwan's work wasn't done. He'd gotten to know me and Chris through the top-prospect summer camps we went to together, and we'd become pretty friendly. It all sort of fit: I was the boisterous one; Chris was the prodigy, happy to let someone else lead the way;

and Juwan was the elder statesman (even though we were all the same age). He was a quieter leader than I was, but definitely an important one all the same. He'd also gotten to know Jimmy King and Ray Jackson, two stars in Texas that Michigan was chasing, and through the recruiting season, after he'd already committed to come to Ann Arbor, he was on the phone checking in on all of us to see what we were thinking, and encouraging us to go through with what had become a crazy plan: to *all* go to the same school.

This went on all the school year. Jimmy and Ray committed to Michigan in the fall. Meanwhile, at Southwestern, with Voshon dominating more fiercely than ever, my own decision started to crystallize. At UNLV, they'd had that scandal with a sports gambler in the hot tub, and it looked like they were headed for NCAA sanctions. Syracuse also had an investigation going on involving Billy Owens and some other players. So staying close to home began to look more and more like the right decision. Even though my idol, Magic Johnson, had gone to Michigan State, it became clear that the place where I'd be able to keep playing as a big point guard (just like Magic) was actually in Ann Arbor, at the University of Michigan, alongside some incredible talent. Most notably, of course, Chris Webber. I remember Chris and I finalized our decision to go to Michigan together when we were at Ed Martin's house one day—after Ed had taken us to ACT prep class. (Yes, he used to do that, too.)

I never even told anyone at Michigan formally. Instead, after our state title game, there was a press conference, and in the afterglow of the win, I just decided to come out with it. Literally a few hours earlier, Chris had had a big press conference to announce he'd made the same decision. He'd worn number 44 in high school, but would switch to number 4 once he got to school, as he was the fourth to sign. I picked number 5. I was the last.

Juwan, Jimmy, Ray, Chris, and Jalen. The consensus was that it was the best draft class in the country. We certainly agreed. Our goal was to win a championship together, and maybe two, three, or, hell, even four. Who knew what could happen from there.

Five guys, one dream.

There are people who will tell you that college sports have always been dirty—that shady things have been going on since way before the Fab Five ever went to Michigan. And they have a point. But the changes that have happened at warp speed over the past several years have accelerated everything. College isn't as much a destination for top recruits anymore—it's more like a tollbooth, a place to fly through on the way to the NBA. When Steve Fisher or Brian Dutcher sat in our living rooms, they were selling us on a program where we were very possibly going to spend four years (or, if we became really good, probably three; ridiculously good, two); where they were going to develop us as players; and where we would be trying to build something together. They were selling our parents on the idea that they would be developing a quality young man and were offering a good education. Finally, they were selling both of us on the notion that all this together would give us the best shot at a professional career.

Today when, say, John Calipari comes to talk to a player about Kentucky, it's just one thing: the pros. He can say that he's had nineteen NBA draft picks over his first five years with the Wildcats (Michigan, my alma mater, hasn't had nineteen first draft picks in the last twenty years!), and if the player comes to play for him, he'll do everything he can to make him the next player who goes right to the pros after one year. The emphasis isn't on building anything or academics. It's about one subject: the player's best route to the NBA to take care of himself and the ones he loves.

Now, let me ask you a question: You just read those two paragraphs. Did you make any value judgments on one versus the other? Did you think to yourself, it's better when college basketball stars go to school for four years rather than leave after just one? Did you think to yourself, it was better when the sneaker companies weren't massive, all-powerful corporations? Did you think that coaches were more genuine when they were recruiting kids for longer stints at school? Do you have this sense that the new world order in college basketball is somehow dirtier?

Maybe you do, maybe you don't—I shouldn't be accusing you of anything. But I think it is fair to say that a lot of people who follow sports, and definitely a lot of people who write and comment on sports like their sports to be pure and virtuous. They like to feel that something like college basketball is part of a greater educational mission. And a big reason they feel that way is that that's how the National Collegiate Athletic Association, the NCAA, sells itself, with graphics and features promoting academic All-Americans during the television broadcasts, and all kinds of other references to scholarships and academics. What they aren't marketing is their billion-dollar deal to televise March Madness. What they don't want you to think is what I told you before: It's all about the money.

Now, I don't have any problem with the truth. Coca-Cola is all about the money. General Motors is all about the money. Why should the sports world—even the college sports world—be any different? Because universities are nonprofits? Tell that to the chancellors who make six and seven figures, and the alumni who get letters every week asking for more donations. I can't say it enough: What drives everything about college sports, and certainly the recruiting, is the money.

Today, more money than ever before.

SONNY VACCARO was the original sneaker guy. Sonny worked for everyone at one point or another—Nike, Adidas, Reebok—and basically created an entire industry based on young basketball players wearing sneakers and, ultimately, the best of them becoming the faces of those brands when they turned pro. Sonny's signature deal was signing Michael Jordan to Nike in 1984, when Jordan left North Carolina for the NBA. And what's most important to understand is how long it took to get that deal done. Not a few days or weeks or even months of negotiations. No, it was years and years of work.

Sonny's job (and he really invented the job) was to connect kids, coaches, and schools with the shoe companies as early as possible. College was a big part of that, but even more so was high school. So he linked up with the schools and coaches that had the best talent—for example, Southwestern and Perry Watson. Southwestern was getting Nike stuff for years before I got there. Remember those white hats I told you about that I saw at the fairgrounds? Well, the Southwestern players also had the matching shoes, big Nikes with the "Nike" written big on the back of the shoes. That was definitely part of the appeal of going there and playing on the team—which of course fed into the winning atmosphere. What—it sounds *dirty* to you? High school kids who couldn't afford sneakers getting free sneakers to play in? What if the theater club was sponsored by a local theater and got costumes to use in their plays? Or the marching band got new snare drums paid for by the city orchestra?

Now, here's the important thing that was different in my day: Southwestern was going to be a Nike school regardless of where any of us went to college. Sonny Vaccaro or Nike wasn't going to be involved in my decision to go to Michigan or wherever. Sonny was doing his job if the best high school players in Detroit were wearing Nike and making Nike cool all throughout the city. That's why they always use that term *grassroots*. It was grassroots basketball and grassroots marketing.

Today, though, it's all changed. The grassroots idea is gone. Today, if a school like Southwestern is a Nike school, and a coach

like Perry Watson is getting gear from Nike, and a top recruit decides to go to an Adidas-sponsored college team, Nike's going to be
upset. They want their player to stay Nike all the way through. They
think of him as one of their employees, or, maybe even more accu-
rately, one of their products. If Nike gets upset, they might decide
not to sponsor Southwestern anymore. Which means no more Nike
gear for Perry's teams, and one less thing to entice a young kid to
come to the school.

Unless of course Adidas comes in after I sign with the Adidas
school, and says, Perry, we'll take care of you, we'll give you Adidas
gear, but keep in mind, your next star had better go to an Adidas
school. Or else you'll be right back where you started.

You see why Perry Watson would rather be on a golf course in
Florida than trying to do right by his players in this atmosphere?

But me? I'm on the other end. I *wish* it had been like this when
I was playing. Because think of who has all the power in that situation: The player. The talent. Here's how I see it: The Superfriends
would have been sponsored by a shoe company starting when I
was twelve. And then I would have been steered into a high school
sponsored by the same company. Once I established myself as a
young star, the shoe company would have given my mom and my
uncles and my brothers tons of free stuff and, hey, if they needed
them, even jobs. They'd send someone to advise me, to get in my
ear, connect me with pro players and even celebrities on the phone,
make me feel great. Probably tell me to "grayshirt," or hold myself
back a year in school, so I got another year of physical growth and
maturity on everyone else, to make me even more dominant as high
school continued. Then the shoe company, through some sort of

fixer or street agent, would have guided me to that one-year college stop-off with a school, and a coach, affiliated with that same sneaker company. And then finally, at the ripe old age of nineteen, when I got drafted, at last I could sign the seven-, eight-, or even nine-figure endorsement deal that I'd been promised, wink-wink, over a handshake, way back when I first hooked up with the company. Oh, right, plus whatever couple of million I'm going to get from my actual NBA team.

It's just like the Wayans brothers used to say on *In Living Color*, right?

Mo' money mo' money mo' money . . .

Really, to me, there's only one thing dirty, or unfair, or unjust about that whole deal. That I can't get paid until I turn pro! Though I'm sure the big companies can find ways to get that money to my family somehow along the way, right?

Ladies and gentlemen, amateurism at its finest!

And we've only barely touched the NCAA.

BEING A top-flight college coach these days is a tricky proposition. Not that it was ever easy to chase the best players and try and recruit them to your program, but now the top talents are just there for one year before they take off on you. If they don't take off on you, in fact, then something went drastically wrong—because that means they weren't as good as you hoped they'd be. Then, of course, you've got everything we just went over—the influence of the shoe companies in everything you do, and all the players you go after.

So after a coach's list of potential recruits gets whittled down based on who's wearing what shoes, the main difference in the recruiting process is that it's a lot less personal than it used to be. Remember, Coach Fisher and Coach Dutcher came to Juwan Howard's grandmother's funeral before he ever played a single game at Michigan. The reason they came was that they legitimately cared about the kid. Believe me, if anything else were the case, we would have seen through it.

Today, the best recruiter in the game is Coach Cal at Kentucky. The best thing about John is that he's not a phony. He's not trying to sell anyone any fake notion of "student-athlete." He treats his program at Kentucky like a trade school: He's going to bring a kid in and train him to be a basketball player. That's how he gets nine McDonald's All-Americans on one roster. It's effective and successful because it's realistic. Kentucky teams remind me of the Fab Five—great players choosing to go to school together and play together.

Today, all college coaches need to speak the kids' language. What are you going to do to keep my pro plans on track? Well, check out our amazing facilities—our weight room, our film room, our lounge. Our barbershop. Our private plane that we take to games. Then there might be other expectations. Like, the player's family wants to move with him to the college town—can the school hook up a job for the dad, or the mom, either in the program or in a local business nearby? You bet they can. That's not a new phenomenon, but it's more prevalent today than it was when I was getting recruited. It has to be. Because there's more money, and more money means more people doing more of whatever they have to do to succeed.

All this change has had a big impact on the college game, and most of all the NCAA Tournament in March. Because you have these top-flight schools stocked with freshman superstars, and then other teams, the midmajors and the somewhat smaller programs, playing with guys who aren't top recruits and therefore stay in school for three and four years. Those schools, lesser-known possible Cinderellas, have a better shot than ever before in the tourney. They're more experienced, and older, and can use those advantages in trying to knock off the freshman phenoms. The dynamic is kind of an unintentional consequence, but it's what's happened all the same.

FINE. EVEN if part of me wishes players could get paid before they actually turn pro, if we're going to be real, we have to acknowledge that there are downsides to everything. Like players getting pampered and treated like stars before they hit puberty. That can't be good for the process of learning how to play well with other stars and how to become a winner. When you're young, you need to be put in your place ... you need to learn the hard way. Like I did getting my butt kicked by Uncle Paramore in video games, getting run through boot camp by Tony Jones, and then learning the game, and the game of life, from Coach Watson. As I said earlier, if I had been around during today's system, who knows what would have happened to my career. And even more important, what would have happened to me in the game of life? The guidance I had at that young age was paramount to my getting to where I am today.

Ultimately, in places like Detroit, it's important to have local influences like Perry. If coaches like him don't have control of their

players, and their teams, then they're not going to be able to maintain the necessary influence to remain leaders at their schools, in
their communities. That influence is central to getting their young
athletes on the path to an education. Dozens and dozens of Perry's
players went on to college. A few got a shot at the pros. More important, many more got other opportunities thanks to the education.
Now, in Detroit today there are no Perry Watsons. There are no
Ed Martins either. There's no one to guide the talent. I'm trying to
offer a counter to the often-bleak reality with the tuition-free charter school I founded there, and there are a few other folks fighting
the good fight with me, but too much has changed for it to ever really go back to what it was.

Beyond just Detroit, the old system was better for the game overall, the majority of the players. Perry Watson was an individual who
could handle the responsibility of getting free stuff from sneaker
companies and also looking out for his kids. Sonny Vaccaro was an
individual who could handle looking to make money for his em-
ployer and also wanting the best for the kids who came to his ABCD
Nike camps. Sonny is a genuine good dude. I still am friends with
him and his wife, Pam. If a kid wasn't going to make it to the pros,
or even a Division I program, Sonny would have been happy to hear
that his camp maybe got the kid a shot at a DII or DIII program.

It always has been all about the money. But in my day, there was
room for a lot more other good stuff as well. That helped raise all
the players up, not just the superstars.

SO WHAT would I change about the recruiting system today?
Well, if a kid can play one year in college, and then get tens of mil-

lions of dollars from a shoe company, who am I to institute some "system" that will prevent a young man who has talent and value in the corporate world from getting what he deserves? But while that may actually be fairer to a young superstar, it's not nearly as good for the guys at the levels below him. That's true in college ball, high school, and AAU competition.

The core issue here is the current age limit, which forces players to go to college for a year and therefore spend another year not getting paid for playing basketball. As I write this, it seems like there's a consensus to raise the limit one more year—to twenty. There will be a bunch of problems with that. And it's also hypocritical, especially since the top four players in the 2015 draft were all nineteen years old.

First, when it was established, the age limit was not for the LeBron Jameses or Kobe Bryants of the world, but for players who don't really have the skills to jump right into the league and succeed. Does anyone really think LeBron or Kobe would have turned out to be better players if they were forced to play in college for a year? Or if Kevin Durant or Carmelo Anthony had to play for two years? Those players aren't the issue.

Also because of the age limit, there's a ton of grayshirting going on. And so after young athletes get held back when they're younger, they graduate from high school as stars when they're nineteen. Some maybe at twenty. So what happens then? Even if they haven't gone to college, should they be eligible to join the pros?

Look, in theory, it's America. There should be no restrictions, and players should be able to do whatever they want—free market. But if I'm trying to make both games—pro and college—better, here's what I say: Make it a rule that if you go to college, you have to stay for two years. Then, as an alternative, also let players opt out completely and declare for the NBA draft out of high school. One or the other—enter the draft, or sign a letter of intent. That lets the next Andrew Wigginses and Jabari Parkers start making money immediately but also protects the next tier of players from their own temptations, assuming they're smart enough to choose college. It'll be on the college coaches to convince them that college for two years is the best choice for them. If not, they'll end up in the NBA Development League, or Europe, and that's not the worst thing.

Let's go back a step to high school and AAU ball. AAU gets a bad rap for a lot of reasons. One is legitimate: the sleazy characters that are involved with programs that seem to pop up out of nowhere, with no affiliation to schools or community centers or churches. It's the Wild West, with guys who care much more about the shoe companies than the interests of kids. Still, don't hate on AAU ball. It's been a core part of competitive development for the best players in the world for generations. So I'd rather we eliminate the bad things that have developed in AAU without sacrificing the good aspects.

Obviously not every coach or teacher is going to be Perry Watson, but the more accountable mentors you put in a kid's life, the better chance they are going to turn out to be better people, and better players. And that's good for everyone—the kids, the parents, and, ultimately, the NCAA and the NBA. Make AAU coaches get certified through the schools, and keep their teams connected to the schools, or churches, or community centers. The best way to make sure that programs are legitimate is to keep them tied to legitimate institutions and leadership. When I was in high school, our Southwestern team had an AAU component that would compete in tournaments. When we went to a national tournament in Vegas, we took Chris Webber with us and the rest of our normal roster. When we played a team of pros from the Soviet Union as seniors, Juwan actually played with us. It all ran through guys like Perry and Tony Jones at Southwestern and other great coaches like Curtis Hervey with the Superfriends, and Rocky Watkins and Glover Ernest at Michigan AAU. All good dudes who had the respect of the community.

The basketball world has evolved a lot in the last twenty-five years. It's still a world that means a lot to me.

After all, the Fab Five revolutionized it.

SECOND QUARTER

Five Times

4 • The Revolution

In March of 2011, when we produced the *Fab Five* documentary for ESPN, the highlight for me wasn't our big rating. Or being recognized for the impact we'd had on basketball and culture. Or even the idea that a whole new generation of kids who'd only kind of heard of us got a chance to see what we were all about. No, to me, the best part, bar none, was the controversy. All the people getting upset about what we said about Duke—including, by the way, my good friend Grant Hill himself, who wrote an op-ed piece in the *New York Times* about it. Yeah, that got the film more attention, which was great. But the real reason I loved it was that it made me feel like people actually hated us again.

In sports, no matter how controversial you are, once enough time passes, the edge disappears, and you go from being divisive to being fondly remembered. Fans who vilified you for what you stood for seem to forget about all that and pretend they always were your biggest supporters. I'm all about the love, and there's nothing I appreciate more than when I get stopped on the street by someone who wants to talk basketball or reminisce about the Final Fours. But to me, the significance of what the Fab Five accomplished lies in the people who *didn't* like us, the people we made uncomfortable, the people who were forced to confront a new reality when we came on the scene. It was nice to have that back for a while.

The most obvious instance of time's dulling the haters in sports is Muhammad Ali. He spent his career taking stands that were unpopular with almost all of America: joining the Nation of Islam and changing his name, refusing to join the army and to go to Vietnam. He paid for it dearly at the time, only to be crowned a "legend" once he retired and began to suffer from Parkinson's disease. By that point he wasn't nearly as threatening as he once was to a lot of people.

Ali actually holds a special place in the hearts of the Fab Five. In 1992, before our first NCAA Tournament game, in Atlanta, it turned out he was staying in the same hotel as us. And at the time, he actually lived in Michigan, on a farm near Lake Michigan, across the state from Detroit. He knew who we were, was a big fan of ours, and wanted to meet us. We were invited to his suite in the hotel, and he was messing around with us there, doing these magic tricks that he kind of became famous for as a way to communicate with people when speaking became difficult. But he could definitely still talk when he really wanted to talk, and he knew our names (Muhammad Ali knew our names! Uncle Paramore would have been impressed), and he gave us a bit of advice. "Don't stop being confident," he said. "Don't stop being cocky. Keep doing exactly what you're doing.

"Go shock the world." Now you see why Jawon went crazy for the cameras, saying, "We gonna shock the world." He also thought we were going on *The Cosby Show,* but that is another subject for another day.

. . .

SIX MONTHS before meeting Ali, I was just heading off to be a star at Michigan. But I felt like Jed Clampett. You know, from *The Beverly Hillbillies.* I was driving my mom's green Dodge Shadow, which I'd gotten late in eleventh grade to replace the Omni she had given me when I got my license. Since my mom worked at Chrysler, we'd gotten both cars on a big discount using the "A-plan" for employees. The car wasn't too big, and I'd loaded up the back with my stereo components, so for the thirty-minute drive west out of Detroit to Ann Arbor, I had to pack it to the brim to get everything I needed for school inside. Like I said, Jed Clampett.

When I got to town, I had no idea where my dorm was and had to call an assistant coach from a pay phone to have him direct me. That's right, no cell phone! Finally, I pulled up and got out. I heard my name being shouted. I looked, and there they all were— Michigan's other four star freshman recruits, hanging out of the window, welcoming the fifth and final member of the club.

It couldn't have felt more right.

I'd obviously known C-Webb for years, and he and I had become friendly with Juwan Howard through camps. We'd met Jimmy King at the McDonald's All-American game the spring before and had actually rearranged our dorm assignments with the other guys so all five of us could all be in connecting rooms. I'd never met Ray Jackson before, though—so this was really the first time, in my head and my heart, that the full brotherhood was formed. Instantly. From the get-go, we were all just giddy, joking around like we'd known each other for years, like we were destined to play together. After an hour or so it became apparent hanging out and playing video games wasn't going to quench the adrenaline that we had going.

If you looked out the window of our dorm rooms, you'd notice a full-court basketball court right outside South Quad. And there's no time like the present, right? So we headed outside and walked onto the court. There were some other kids playing and they were psyched to have us join them, pretty quickly figuring out who we were. At first, we played against them a bit, going easy. Soon, though, it turned into a highlight show. I threw an alley-oop to Chris, and he almost broke the basket dunking it. Jimmy and Ray started taking turns going coast-to-coast. Juwan, throwing bullet outlet passes, and two-handed stuffs. Total Showtime. The other guys who had been playing stood off to the side, egging us on to do more. Pretty soon people were hanging out of windows all over the quad, checking us out, screaming for us, giving us love.

Unofficially, it was the first day of the Fab Five.

It was the first sign that a revolution might be coming.

A COUPLE of weeks later, it was time for the Wolverine fitness test. Before you could be cleared to practice, you had to complete a run of a certain distance in a given amount of time, depending on your position. (Guards had to run faster than forwards and centers.) To be honest, I didn't know how far we were going to have to run, either because they hadn't told us or because I didn't remember. I just knew to show up at the track on this one afternoon, and we'd go from there.

If only it were so simple. Because while the five of us had pretty much become inseparable over those first few weeks of school, none of us had really gotten the lay of the land of the campus, meaning we had no idea where the track was. Furthermore, we were college freshmen, and if anyone knows anything about college freshmen, it's that they have no idea how to manage their time. So we went back to our dorm after classes, changed clothes, and then tried to figure out our way to the track. That didn't work, so we piled into a cab. Fortunately the driver knew the way, and we got there with a minute to spare. As we walked up to the group, Coach Fisher was definitely giving us dirty looks for almost being late.

I remember I had my bag in one hand and a sandwich in the other. I'd been in class all day and hadn't gotten a chance to eat anything until we were out of that cab. Meanwhile, all around us, the upperclassmen were stretching and almost salivating, as if they couldn't wait to watch us huff and puff our way around the track. Rob Pelinka, a junior guard (and future NBA agent to the stars), had won the run the couple of years prior, and the guys were saying that he was going to toast everyone again. But there was one thing they didn't know: At Southwestern, you couldn't play basketball for Perry Watson if you didn't run cross-country. So I'd been running like this for four years. Whether it was a one-mile run, or a five-mile run, or whatever (it turned out to be a mile and a half), this wasn't going to be a problem for me.

Sure enough, with Pelinka as my measuring stick the whole time, I cruised in ahead of him, and far ahead of everyone else. Wasn't even breathing heavy. And let's just say the scene afterwards wasn't exactly cool, calm, and collected. Chris, Juwan, Jimmy, and Ray were whooping and hollering—climbing on my back like we'd just won the NCAA title. Chanting my name, not caring about the looks we were getting from everyone else. All the adrenaline that had been pumping since we'd gotten to campus, ever since we'd signed with Michigan, really, was pouring out.

And we hadn't even walked into the gym yet.

. . .

COMPETITION ISN'T a bad thing. Competition is what makes companies money. Competition is what gets kids into Ivy League schools. Competition encourages excellence. So the idea of us being concerned about what the upperclassmen on the basketball team thought of us when we came on board wasn't high on our agenda. We didn't hate them; we didn't resent them. They were our teammates, and we were looking forward to playing with them. But because of the way we'd been recruited, we saw ourselves as a group. And because of our commitment to one another, we were planning to prove that we were the best players on the team, which we got a chance to do on our very first day of scrimmages.

In the fall, before official practices with coaches and drills, the team would do workouts on our own in the gym. When basketball players get a chance to work out on their own, that's basically an open invitation for pickup games. So on that first day in the gym, with twelve or thirteen of us there, the upperclassmen started dividing everyone up into teams. Which is when I spoke up.

"What about us against you?"

Huh?

"Freshmen against all y'all. Our five against your best five."

One, I was thinking that all we wanted to do was play together again, just like we had on that outdoor court in South Quad. Two, because there were more than ten guys in the gym, I was also concerned not all of us would get picked, and one of us would have to sit out the first run. Three, as far as my own situation went, I knew one thing I loved about playing with our five was that I was the point guard. In high school, Howard Eisley had run our offense. Here, with my new teammates, I could be like two of my idols— Magic and Steve Smith—big at the point, running the show. And last, most important, I was thinking, *Well, yeah, this is a pretty quick and straightforward way to prove how good we are together.*

Maybe a little reluctantly, the sophomores, juniors, and seniors agreed. But, hey, this was also a chance for them to put us right in our place. Five games later—after who knows how many alley-oops, fast-break dunks, threes drilled from way out; you name it, we hit it—I'm not sure they were thrilled with their choice. Because we dominated them. We won every game.

And, yes, we were going crazy the whole way, screaming at each other, talking trash, pumping ourselves up with every basket and great play. But, ultimately, regardless of all that, the upperclassmen had no choice but to accept the result. Because that's what competition forces you to do. Once real practices started, and the coaches started dividing us up in different ways, competition revealed the same fact again and again. The freshmen were the ones distinguishing themselves as the best players on the team.

That left the coaches with a decision to make.

I'LL SAY this a bunch of times, and sound like an old man doing it: You have to remember how different college basketball was twenty-some years ago. Picking up from what I talked about in the last chapter, it wasn't a one-year stop on the way to the pros. Lots of the best players stayed in school all four years. Almost all stayed three years. Which meant you could develop kids, bring them along, and move them through a system. I mean, before 1972, freshmen weren't even allowed to play on varsity teams in the NCAA.

But Steve Fisher and Brian Dutcher and their recruiting staff took the first step toward a new era when they were able to convince five of the best prospects in the country to all come to Ann Arbor in the fall of 1991. They weren't trying to revolutionize the system. They were just hoping to save their jobs. Two years earlier, Coach Fisher had had a really strange experience—which started when Bill Frieder, the longtime Michigan head coach, had announced late in the 1988–89 season that he would be leaving after the NCAA Tournament to go coach at Arizona State. Well, that didn't sit well with Bo Schembechler, the Wolverine football coach and athletic director—a true "Michigan Man" if there ever was one—who saw Frieder's move as disloyal, and fired him before the tournament, elevating Steve Fisher to the top job. So then what happened? Steve led Glen Rice, Rumeal Robinson, and company to the championship. It was an incredible job of coaching, but it also raised expectations just a little bit in Ann Arbor. And when Michigan was bounced out of the tournament in the second round the next year, and then had a losing record the year after that, he was in trouble. Until he made his Hail Mary pass and got us.

The staff knew they were going to have a situation to handle once we got to campus—because, very simply, we were brought in to improve the team, and, eventually, replace the players who had underperformed the previous year. But as confident and cocky as we were, even we didn't expect to all start as freshmen. It just wasn't the way things were done. So nothing was set in stone—and with the new faces meeting the old ones, that could have been a recipe for disaster.

Particularly since the guys on our team weren't bums—they were good players. I mentioned Rob Pelinka. Mike Talley, a junior guard, had been Mr. Basketball in Michigan two years ahead of me and Chris—he had played against me at Cooley, Southwestern's big rival. Mike drove a silver Mustang around campus with a Raiders logo on the hood. Definitely cooler than my Shadow. Eric Riley had been one of the best rebounders and shot blockers in a really strong Big Ten Conference the year before we got there. Huge stud. They weren't good players—they were great players. How were they supposed to feel with these freshmen coming in and running and dunking past everyone?

In the end, there were a few reasons why our team didn't implode before we even had a chance to get going, and why the upperclassmen stood with us once our story took off. One, the head coach. Steve Fisher, who I'm still very tight with to this day, was the perfect blend of stern and flexible. To this day, Steve; his wife, Angie; and their son, Mark, are among the best people I've met in my life. Good coaches need to adjust to their players. They know everybody's different, and know how to nurture players in different ways. They don't need to show the media how strict they are, and they also don't need to bend over backwards to gain the approval of their players. Even today—after he's had so much success at San Diego State, developing an NBA Finals MVP like Kawhi Leonard— Steve still doesn't get enough credit for being a great coach. He's not in the buddy network that way. But then, and now, Steve knew exactly what he was doing and set the right kind of tone for our locker room. He wasn't afraid to give us, the players, a large measure of control of the situation. Remember, I had been on winning teams my whole life. I had played with other great players before. I knew, even as a freshman, ways to deal with that in the locker room. The amount of joking you do, the kinds of things you say and don't say to older players, the ways you bond, the lines you don't cross, all that stuff. That went back to following the lead of Uncle Paramore, really—being cool with everyone in a room, knowing how to be outgoing and friendly.

But, really, I bring it all back to that first day in the gym, and even before that, that day on the track. We showed up, we acted like we were the best, and we proved it. The competition was healthy, because the truth was to be found in what happened when we competed. Was instantly setting ourselves apart and challenging the upperclassmen dangerous? Maybe—but it also left them no grounds to ever say that the coaching staff was playing favorites. To their everlasting credit, Riley, Pelinka, James Voskuil, even Talley (who probably had the toughest time of anyone) all did an incredible job of welcoming us into the fold, supporting us, and being great teammates. That held true when the coaching staff inserted Chris, Juwan, and me into the starting lineup at the beginning of the season, moving three upperclassmen to the bench. And then, a few weeks later, when Mike Talley got in trouble for missing a meeting, Jimmy followed. And ultimately, in February, a little more than halfway through the season against Notre Dame on national TV, Ray became the fifth.

By then, no one would be able to call it hype.

· · ·

FOR ME, everything in college was an extension of everything I'd come from. The trash-talk, the emotional play, being a leader on the team—that was all who I was as a kid at Southwestern, on display in front of a bigger audience. And so were the shorts.

I always liked my shorts longer than they were meant to be. For one, baggy clothes were in style in general, and I always wanted my image on the basketball court to be stylish—like anyone who takes pride in dressing well, it made me feel confident, and good about myself, and that helped my game. At UNLV, they had longer shorts than other teams, as did Syracuse with Derrick Coleman, and Illinois with Marcus Liberty, as did the Bulls in the NBA. So I wasn't the only one who liked the look of long shorts, or to realize that longer shorts were more comfortable.

Not that I had too much experience playing with the perfect pair of shorts. In high school, while Nike sponsored Southwestern's program and gave us game shoes, they didn't provide uniforms. You would try to get guys who came back from college to give you their shorts for pickup runs, but for high school, long shorts weren't possible. So I'd pull down the short shorts the school gave me as low as I could, and then pull my shirt out to cover them up. This became an issue with our principal, Ms. Hines, who brought me into Coach Watson's office at one point and said to both of us, "Look, if you don't stop sagging your pants, you will not play on the basketball team." Well, I needed to come up with some solution to this ridiculous problem, so I actually started wearing another pair of shorts underneath my game shorts. No, not compression shorts (this was before they were popular), but actually another pair of gym shorts. They were longer, and let me rest my game shorts a little lower, on top of them. Weird solution, yes, but problem sort of solved.

At Michigan, I was ready to deal with the same issue. The first thing I did when they handed out practice gear was what I did in high school: I riffled through the pile of shorts and took the biggest pair. They were intended for one of the biggest players on the team—six-foot-ten, 260-pound Chip Armer. And Chip, thankfully, wasn't as fashion-conscious as I was, and was okay with trading shorts, even if mine were a little small on his frame. That took care of practice. The next step was convincing Coach Fisher to talk to Nike, who sponsored the whole program, about ordering us longer shorts. All of us were into the idea, so we all worked to do some convincing, and Coach ultimately agreed to get them made for us.

And somewhere back in Detroit, watching the games on TV, I'm sure Ms. Hines, my old principal, winced when she saw us take the court.

FIVE FRESHMEN. In 1991–1992, the notion that freshmen could play major roles on one of the top teams in the country was a big deal in college basketball. We were ranked twenty-fifth at the start of the season, essentially based on sheer speculation of what people thought we could do, and that got us a lot of attention with the national media. That's when they first started throwing around the term "Fab Five." We didn't love that name—we felt like it was plagiarism, considering hip-hop legend Fab 5 Freddy had pioneered the term. (Of course, the media had never heard of Fab 5 Freddy, so they didn't know the phrase was out there.) Anyway, we originally had a different name for ourselves. We wanted it to be "Five Times." As in, five times one equals five, five of us as one. Yeah, I'm thinking the same thing you are. I'm glad it didn't stick.

No matter the hype, winning was why we stayed relevant, even before our run in the tournament. We peaked when ranked eleventh in January, sat at fifteen when Ray became the fifth freshman starter in February, and were right around the same when we entered the NCAAs. That's pretty good considering how deep college basketball was at the time. Kansas under Roy Williams, UCLA under Jim Harrick, and Kentucky under Rick Pitino were all great teams. In the Big Ten, Indiana had Calbert Cheaney, Ohio State had Jim Jackson, and Michigan State was strong with Shawn Respert. But, really, the reason we exploded on the scene, the reason we became not just famous, but infamous, even before our run in March Madness, was *how we played.* That story line became national news from the outset because our fifth game of the year was played on national television, in front of a huge audience, against the number-one team in the country: the Duke Blue Devils.

Any team I was ever on, I was a loud presence—full of will, determination, and brashness. That brashness was supplemented by the sense of destiny I had—the feeling that because my dad was an NBA star, I belonged to the club already. That in turn helped me become a pretty influential guy in any locker room I ever was a part of, right on all the way through the pros. People gravitate toward those who are confident and comfortable—and they also tend to follow those who speak their mind. Chris, Juwan, Jimmy, and Ray were obviously comfortable playing in the loud, brash, fearless, unapologetic style that we established in that very first practice. It fit them well, and bonded us closer together as a group. But I think any of them who were there would agree—they followed my lead.

In that Duke game, all of my emotions came together in a way that turned brashness into something that looked a whole lot like anger.

To understand that game you have to understand that in the beginning of my life, I didn't know what I didn't have. One day, around eighth grade, I was riding with Curtis Hervey to a scrimmage that was at Detroit Country Day. To our left was Cass Lake. I looked out and saw all these people on their Jet Skis and boats. Wow, people jet skiing in Detroit! I didn't know people could do that. Right then, I started realizing what I didn't have and what I would have to do to get it. Take the harder path. Hustle for things, like my Uncle P. Work my butt off, like everyone in my family.

Duke summoned images of all the lakes with people jet skiing on them that I'd ever driven by. And all the teams I'd played growing up that had been able to afford matching bags and warm-up suits, and plane tickets for lots of fans to travel far to see them. For me, Duke wasn't just the number one–ranked team in the country. They were the team I had always played against. And always relished beating the most.

Duke didn't recruit me, and I never would have been interested in going there. These days, I have a lot of respect for Mike Krzyzewski, but as a player, I did not fit their mold. Nor was I interested in trying to. Duke was a place where, in my eyes, kids had taken the easy path. It was especially easy to work up that envy leading up to that game in December of 1991, considering who I was going to be looking at across the floor: Grant Hill. I hadn't forgotten that AAU game five years earlier when he showed up with the brand-new shoes, new sweats, new bags, and, it turned out, a much better team. Now here we were again, and I was hyped. I had circled the date on my calendar from the minute I'd seen the schedule, been talking up the Duke game to my teammates, all that. To top it off, just a few months before, I'd watched Duke beat one of my favorite teams, UNLV, in the tournament. Now I was getting a chance for vengeance.

If you were to read my mind at the time, and listen in to my conversations with my teammates, you would have come across the words "Grant Hill" and "Uncle Tom," a term that people used to refer to other blacks who, it was assumed, had forgotten where they came from and acted like they were white. Would I use that term today to refer to someone? No. Would I even think it? No. Today I'm mature enough to know that successful black people, getting an education, earning money, and wearing nice clothes, are not acting white. They are becoming successful. But at age eighteen, I was coming from a very different place. And it provided great fuel for the adrenaline I needed to compete.

Deep inside, I was jealous of Grant Hill. Of his dad, who went to Yale and played in the NFL. Of his mom, who was college roommates with Hillary Clinton. During a game, if he made a good pass, or the right play, the announcers would say, "Another piece of great fundamentals from Grant Hill," or, "Once again, there's Grant Hill, being a great teammate." When they called my games (even back to high school), I never got that kind of praise, no matter how good the pass was, how passionate the defense was, or how fundamental the play was. It was all just more weight on the chip on my shoulder.

Along with Grant, the All-Americans on that Duke team were two white guys, Christian Laettner and Bobby Hurley. I knew Bobby Hurley's dad was the coach of one of the best high school teams in the country, and that was something I could respect. Still, before I got to college, I think I had one white teammate. One, in all of my school and AAU teams. White people lived in other places, where the houses were bigger, the yards were prettier, and the wallets were thicker. That was a fact of life for me. While college, with the white teammates and thousands of white students around me, was starting to open up my eyes to a new perspective, as a freshman I was predisposed to resent a player like Christian Laettner, and to think he was an "overrated pussy," as I said in the documentary. (Even though, as I learned on the floor, he was a total stud.)

Consider what all the media and publicity and hype injected into the game as well. The black knights versus the white knights. I mean, our rosters were almost the reverse of each other: their stars were white, with blacks in supporting roles; our stars were black, with whites in supporting roles. Then there was the long shorts versus the short shorts; the idea that they were disciplined and we were hot dogs; and so on. Forget any resentment I had, it was the story line all the writers scripted for us.

And we loved it. We loved being the rebels, the upstarts, the "Who are they's?" and the "Who do they think they are's?" It fit our collective personality perfectly. Reading cute little stories about this new "Fab Five" in September was cool, but seeing the writers' faces when they came into our locker room, and N.W.A and Public Enemy and the Geto Boys were blasting, was better. Even before Muhammad Ali himself told us to, we wanted nothing more than to shock the world. That was the most fun. That most strengthened our brotherhood. That compelled us to play hard.

We fell way behind in the first half of the game that afternoon, and then clawed our way back, basket by basket, in the second. And we did it our way—loudly and brashly—the same way we'd been doing it since our first day together at Michigan. We weren't going to back down to anyone. Dunks, runners, threes, alley-oops—we threw everything at them. Late in the game, Laettner and I came together fighting for the ball. He thought I would give it up after the whistle—and even started laughing. You see why it wasn't hard to hate him on the court. Anyway, he didn't end up with the ball. Then we had a chance to win it at the buzzer, missed it, and it went to overtime, where Duke ultimately prevailed. It was like *Rocky*— we'd gone the distance with the champ but had come up a bit short.

At Crisler Arena, it was as exciting as any game any Michigan fan had ever seen.

FROM THAT game on, everything took off: the attention we got, the focus on us, how we played, everything. The story line took us right back to another matchup with Duke in the national title game four months later. But before then we still had a lot of growing to do on the basketball court, and the Big Ten schedule gave us that opportunity. The Big Ten then was as strong as it's ever been. I mentioned Calbert Cheaney, the Big Ten's all-time leading scorer, playing for Bob Knight at Indiana, and Jimmy Jackson at Ohio State. Glenn Robinson, a future number-one overall draft pick, was at Purdue. Michael Finley was putting in work at Wisconsin. My old teammate Voshon Lenard was starting to do things at Minnesota. Michigan State with Shawn Respert and Coach Jud Heathcote was a top-twenty team. Illinois and Iowa had great coaching under Lou Henson and "Dr. Tom" Davis, respectively. We went 11-7 in the Big Ten. No game was easy. Once the ball was tipped, we were just another quality squad playing for the W.

Of course, in the eyes of the media, it wasn't so simple. The more they saw us, the less they knew what to do with us. The aspect of our style of play that shocked them more than anything else: trash-talking.

Let's go back for a little history lesson. First off, people have been trash-talking since the very beginning of sports. Babe Ruth calling his shot, that was good trash-talking right there. Satchel Paige was one of the all-time great trash-talkers. Obviously Ali. And in basketball, Michael Jordan and Larry Bird were two of the best trash-talkers the NBA has ever known. So it's not like the Fab Five invented the art.

I came to Michigan having been an all-around student of trash-talking almost since I could talk at all. The video game marathons at Uncle Paramore's house were my initial education. Then I got to use what I learned out in the street as I learned to play basketball and other sports. As I grew up, and got into AAU and high school ball, I realized what trash-talking could do for me. I realized that it could elevate me to the next level.

For me, trash-talking was a way to get into my opponent's head, get him off his game, and give me an edge. Hitting a shot, great. Hitting a shot and screaming about it and letting the other guy know I was going to hit the next one, too—more than great. It was the tool I used to get myself in the zone I needed to be in to play the best I could. Think of it like this: If I had to play the game in silence, I wouldn't have been as good. The adrenaline just wouldn't have been there. God bless Barry Sanders and Derrick Rose and players who can get themselves to the level they need to get to without talking or emoting. I'm not one of them. In fact, to this day, the only way I can lift myself to that level is by getting emotional, by expressing myself, by trash-talking.

I put in a guide to trash-talking at the end of this chapter, for all the people out there who need a few friendly tips. For me, the key was not holding back. I would say pretty much anything I needed to. You remember Acie Earl, who played for Iowa? He was built kind of funny, reminding me of how my sister was built. (No offense, Tam!) So I told him that, over and over again. I'd scream at coaches, right at Bobby Knight and Roy Williams and whoever else as I ran past on the court. I'd use language that I would never use off the court. Between the lines, I thought anything was fair game. If you ask them about playing me in college, Grant Hill and his Duke teammate Thomas Hill will probably tell you that during games, in the heat of battle, I called them "house niggas." All I'll say about that is we used the term plenty of other times against plenty of other players.

If you're a businessman, and you go to work, and you do whatever you have to do to make money, including firing people, or putting another company out of business, no one accuses you of being a bad person. If you're a lawyer, and you defend someone accused of a crime, you don't get labeled as evil. My point is: My job, from AAU to high school to college to the pros, was to do everything I could to play my best, and win. That's it. And a central part of my arsenal—as much as my first step to my left, my three-pointer, my floater—was my ability to trash-talk, to get in my opponent's head, raise my own game in the process, and give my team the best chance to win.

At Michigan, all of us trash-talked. Within the Fab Five, it was as much trash-talking each other as trash-talking the other team. "Hey, he can't stop you!" "Lock him up!" That kind of dialogue. That would be our way of putting us more in sync as a unit, getting the fans pumped up, getting the other team rattled. Whatever we were saying, we were pretty demonstrative about it. That didn't change whether we were on the concrete court at South Quad, an arena with ten thousand people in it, or, in the case of a title game, a stadium with sixty thousand. Once all five of us were playing together for the majority of every game, our ongoing "conversation" and all the chest bumps and high fives and slaps that went along with it were on full display. Five guys egging each other on, feeding off each other's energy. It came to be as much a part of our game as how we shot, passed, and rebounded.

People criticized us and, in the next breath, praised Duke, Kentucky, Kansas for "playing like a team," "playing cohesively," "playing together," and so forth. Which begs just one question:

Then what the hell were we doing?

THE SEASON went on, and it felt like we got bigger with every game. At Michigan, we were huge. Everywhere else, our following was growing. Kids, students, peers, they'd stop us in airports and hotels and scream for us in arenas. Fans for other teams booed us louder than other teams, but you could tell they got us. They understood what our attitude and style were about. They wouldn't have been doing that for just any other team.

Inside our locker room, and inside our dorm rooms, the Fab Five got closer as a unit as the season went on. We all had our roles in the group, with our different personalities. We also had our own nicknames. Juwan was "Nook"—always the most mature—that came from the upbringing he'd gotten from his grandmother. I never saw him without a perfect haircut, or without a crease in his pants. We called Ray "Money," because he was there every time we needed him on the court. He'd make any sacrifice necessary—playing a reserve role if we needed it, matching up against any guard or forward, making an extra pass. He had the most versatility—size, speed, whatever. Off the court, he used to like to fly under the radar. Jimmy was "Jim-Jam." He could run, jump, and glide through the air. He had the Michael Strahan gap in his teeth. Real slick, always showing up clean. Cleaner than me. Jimmy and I developed probably my deepest friendship, largely owing to the fact that we wanted to hang out and kick it more than everybody else. My nickname was the same as it was in high school, "Jinx," just like Sir Jinx, Ice Cube's DJ. Because I used to predict things that came true. And then there was C-Webb, "The Truth." He and I obviously went back the furthest, though I will say that while we all had other friends (like Juwan's boy Lamont "Juice" Carter, who practically lived with us), Chris was the one member of the group who hung out a bit more with other people. That was totally cool but set him apart a bit.

On the court, we were pretty much as good as advertised. Chris was, instantly, one of the best players in college basketball. Juwan was a top-notch big man from the start. Jimmy and Ray were as athletic and skilled as any two players on any court in the country. The way it worked out, I was actually our leading scorer. My best game of the season came out of what should have been a lowlight. I was late for a meeting before our Big Ten opener, away against Iowa, and Coach Fisher benched me (as he should have). We went down early, though, so I ended up going in three minutes after the tip. I never came out, and scored thirty-four, my college career high, in a big win. The boos never sounded so good.

It was apparent that we were making an impact on the younger demo, but the old guard wasn't so into it. Announcers. Writers. Even the referees hated on us. I remember there were these two Big Ten refs, Ed Hightower and Jim Burr. Ed retired just a few years ago, but Jim's still reffing out there today. When we would see them out on the floor before a game, we knew, guaranteed, one of us was going to end up with two fouls before the first TV timeout. I remember one game against Northwestern, when we had a good play on a fast break and, typically, were pumped up afterwards. The other team called a timeout, and as we brought our stools out for the huddle, Hightower came over, pointed to me, and said to Coach, "If this guy smiles again, or laughs, I'm gonna give him a technical foul and throw him out of the game." For what? For smiling? For laughing?

For playing the game the way we played it?

IT WAS definitely generational. But I think it's obvious that the central piece of the puzzle was, is, and always will be race. The contrast between Duke and Michigan was based on that. The shock value of our trash-talking, and our demonstrative style of play, was based on that. People didn't have any problem in *Hoosiers* when the farm boys celebrated all over the court as they made their way through the state tournament. But when we did the same thing, we looked a lot different, and a lot of people—including the folks who were writing about us, and commentating on our games— didn't know how to handle that.

Our style was an extension of how we'd played in high school. If you had gone to a game like Southwestern versus Cooley, you would have seen a lot of the same style of play. But there, it was mostly black players playing in front of mostly black crowds. Now the audience was made up of a completely different demographic. During games, my jersey would get pulled to the side, and the tattoo I had gotten on my chest after my senior year of high school would peek out. The people watching didn't know what to do with that, because very few people in mainstream culture had tattoos back then. I'd wear my diamond (okay, fine, they were cubic zirconia specials) earrings in the press conferences and during interviews. People didn't know what to do with a black college basketball player wearing earrings. We weren't the first group to do all this, but we were the first group a lot of people noticed. All of our shaved heads (except Juwan, who would never get his head shaved—pretty-boy props) represented something to people, something they weren't so comfortable with. Believe me, they were calling us thugs long before the word got tossed around with Richard Sherman (Compton-born, Stanford grad) or any other black star from today's sports world.

It wasn't like we were inventing all this style on our own. We were following the hip-hop artists whose songs we listened to, and whose videos we watched, and whose music told stories that we could relate to and tap into. Hip-hop wasn't mainstream the way it is today, but it was starting to explode. And we saw ourselves as an extension of what it was about. Personally, I felt like basketball was my way of getting to the same level of prominence as those artists. On the court, I told myself I was a "nigga with an attitude."

We were also following in the footsteps of the teams at UNLV, who'd embraced their renegade, outlaw image and ridden it all the way to a national title. (And they were following in the footsteps of another of my favorite teams, John Thompson's Georgetown Hoyas.) Though for us, I think the key was in the contrast. We weren't out on the Strip in Vegas (or in a big city like Washington); we were representing the heartland of the country in Michigan. Which meant that once we stepped out and did our thing, we had to own it. And we absolutely owned it.

A generation earlier, basketball had been a very urban game. In the '60s and '70s, it was closely associated with the playground style as Dr. J and the ABA took the reins of where the sport was going. And right after that, related or not, there had been a downturn, in part due to drugs, but undeniably also based on the fact that the game was considered to be too black to appeal to a widespread white audience. Then, in the '80s, the popularity of the game was transformed, with black superstars like Magic Johnson and Michael Jordan transcending race with their wholesome images. And Larry Bird, a white superstar, right next to them.

Well, in the middle of America's heartland, who came along next, to give the sport its next turn forward? Us. Five black kids who played a certain way—and didn't apologize for it. We were young enough not to care about the haters, close enough to know that we had one another's backs, and good enough to win games and therefore matter in the big picture.

Now, when you talk about race, and racism, you always have to consider the fact that you're usually talking about two different kinds of people and their thoughts. First are the overt racists. The people who sent letters to Ann Arbor, letters in which they called us the n-word, and the c-word, and whatever other words they fancied. Coach Fisher would show us those letters, to fire us up, and to let us know that he took as much offense to them as we did.

But those dummies (and they are dummies ... some put their home addresses on the envelopes) are on the fringe; they're not driving the national conversation. The people who are doing that are not overtly racist. They would probably swear to that on a Bible. But what they are is not knowledgeable. Not educated. They don't know how to react to black players with tattoos and earrings, who listen to hip-hop music, who wear baggy clothes. It's foreign to them, and it's even threatening. And they respond accordingly—which, when they're in the media, means writing columns and articles or talking on the radio or on television about how we don't play the game the right way, we don't represent the University of Michigan the way it should be represented, or whatever.

Think about it: How many black journalists and editors were there in the early '90s? Almost none. There wasn't any Internet, so you had to go by what was written in newspapers and magazines and said on radio and TV shows, and that was it. And there was no way to question it. You couldn't tweet to the radio station or send an e-mail to the newspaper. So all the young people who were energized by us, all the kids who suddenly were Michigan fans and college basketball fans, didn't have an outlet to be heard. Who did? The writers and columnists and talk-show hosts were all old, and white, and clueless about what it all represented.

Last point here: We were also part of the equation. We weren't helpless victims. We were stirring the pot as much as we could. We may not have understood where the media were coming from, but we didn't want to either. We liked being disliked, being misunderstood, being portrayed as rebels. We reveled in that identity. I think a lot of our fans did, too. So if reporters came into the locker room and we were listening to rap music, if anything, we would turn up the volume. I wasn't going to cover up my tattoo; I was going to pull on my jersey a little bit to loosen it so the tattoo showed more. I was definitely going to put on my earrings before every press conference. I was going to scream louder after every shot, talk more trash after every play, puff my chest out farther after every win.

I have no regrets whatsoever.

WE ACTUALLY needed a little winning streak at the end of the season to make sure we got into the NCAA Tournament. That's how tough the Big Ten was. We beat Indiana, ranked two in the nation, at home, and then defeated Purdue on the road and Illinois to finish the regular season 20-8. (No conference tournament then.) We thought we deserved a high seed, considering we'd beaten six ranked teams over the course of the season, and almost knocked off Duke in that early game, but the committee gave us a six-seed, which of course we used as fuel for our fire heading into the tournament.

We beat John Chaney's Temple Owls in the first round, and then East Tennessee State, a Cinderella that had upset Arizona, in the second. Then, at Rupp Arena in Lexington, Kentucky, one of the most hallowed places in all of college basketball—whose all-white Wildcat team had lost to an all-black starting five from Texas Western for the national title in 1966—we got past an Oklahoma State team with Byron Houston and Bryant "Big Country" Reeves. And two nights later, against the Ohio State team that had beaten us in both of our Big Ten matchups earlier in the season, we won in overtime to get to the Final Four. Cut down the nets, the whole nine.

Our opponent in the national semifinal game was Cincinnati, a team that was actually a lot like us. Bob Huggins has always been known as a coach who takes chances on some rough, tough kids, and his team that year was led by big Corie Blount and Nick Van Exel, the point guard who liked to talk just as much trash as we did. And some other guy on their team in the week leading up to the game said something to reporters about how he was going to deal with us, and not let us talk to them. Well, we did plenty of talking, and turned a three-point halftime deficit around, beating them 76–72, to get to the final against our familiar nemesis, the Duke Blue Devils. Still the number one team in the country, and who by this time hated us as much as we hated them.

The first half, we played good basketball. We stayed in the game, we were executing, we were playing hard, making plays out on the floor to keep the game competitive. At halftime, we were actually up a point—no one remembers that! What they remember is what ultimately mattered: In the second half, they smacked us. They took it up to another level. They played like champions. They were the better team, and they won. Competition, remember? It settles everything. Duke was tremendous—back-to-back champs—no shame in losing to them.

Tracing back to sophomore year of high school, it was the fourth straight year I had made at least the final of the biggest tournament there was. I'd won two championships and lost two. So that wasn't anything new. Now, coming up one game short of a national title—one half, really—gave me something new to shoot for.

But I didn't realize how different, and how much more complicated, everything was about to become.

JALEN'S FRIENDLY GUIDE TO TRASH-TALKING

1. **Respect your opponent.** Recognize how good they are, and what it's going to take to beat them.

2. **Be prepared to deal with the consequences.** Because there will be consequences.

3. **Nothing is out of bounds.** But cursing's overrated.

4. **Do your research.** It pays off.

5. **Win.** It's the ultimate final word.

5. ● Nut Check

In the movies, the sequel is almost never as good as the original. On the big screen, you can't capture the same magic the second time around, the same sense of energy and uniqueness that comes with experiencing something for the first time. In real life, it's even rarer.

After we lost to Duke in the 1992 title game, the Fab Five were tighter than ever, thanks to all we'd gone through since we'd shown up in Ann Arbor the previous fall. We also were a better basketball team than we'd ever been. We'd proved not only to be five great recruits, but also five members of a team that blended together perfectly. Our skills meshed, our talents meshed, and we just had one goal: to win. Our box scores from freshman and sophomore years are split pretty evenly. One game it might be C-Webb who had the points, but another game it might be me, or Juwan, or sometimes Jimmy. Whoever had the hot hand, or had the best matchup, got the ball, and the results bore themselves out in the success.

We had a name for our shared fight. Every time we took the floor, we didn't say "Win on 3," or "Defense," but "One, Two, Three . . . NUT CHECK!" It was a reference to what we called "checking our nuts," or checking our ego on and off the floor. We got the phrase from a Geto Boys record called "Gotta Let Your Nuts Hang." And used it constantly to keep each other in line: "You're not practicing hard ... you're late for training table ... you say you're going to do something, but you're not doing it ... We were gonna go out at 10:00 ... we're still looking for you at 11:15, 11:30 ... You got to check your nuts." It was our own little code, our signal of brotherhood and absolute togetherness.

And in our Fab Five sequel, we were going to need it more than ever.

NOW, WHILE I wouldn't say we had the most normal college experience, I also don't want to let anyone think that we didn't go to college. In our day, becoming part of the campus community was part of being a college basketball star. We didn't have the same life as a kid who came to study law or chemistry and join a frat, but we definitely went to college.

In the beginning, I decided to be really proactive in class, to send the message to the professor and other students that I was for real. In Southwestern, I'd always made the honor roll and taken pride in not being a dumb jock. So in my first few big lectures, I sat up front, asked questions, and tried to be involved. Well, it didn't take too long for me to hear the snickers of other people in the class, whispering things like "Oh, isn't that cute—the basketball player wants to be a student." Really, I was just adjusting like any other freshman, but immediately, my adjustments were going under a microscope. I didn't speak up too much after that. I went back to my style of getting my work done under the radar, and making the dean's list, quietly.

Back in our dorm rooms, just like any other kids, we spent a ton of time playing video games. This was the Nintendo and Sega Genesis era, and our top games were Tecmo Bowl and Madden. Just like being at Uncle Paramore's house, the trash-talking that took place during those games was epic—and perfect practice for the court. As athletes, we had to make it competitive. We kept records of who won what game, who owed money to whom from our bets, and who was up next in our circuit. We had a shutout rule: If you went down 21-zip at halftime in Madden, say, the game was over. No mercy.

We went out just like other students on Saturday nights. We played beer pong at fraternities or headed to parties at the Union, the center of campus life at Michigan. I'll never forget trying to sneak a forty into the Union freshman year. I had it in the pocket of my sweats, and it slipped out onto the steps and shattered. I just kept walking as if no one had noticed that the starting point guard of the Fab Five now had beer spilled halfway up his pants. You won't find that little episode on any "Champagning and Campaigning" greatest-hits reels.

It's interesting to look back on the whole racial element of what we were going through socially. At the same time as the Fab Five's national profile was giving us a crash course on the racial divide of our country in the early '90s, we were going to a school that had a diverse, but largely white, student body. For me, it was the first time I was interacting with white people on a day-to-day basis. And learning how to play beer pong with some guys at Zeta Beta Tau represented a way more positive experience than getting taunted by opposing fans on the road.

Still, we weren't regular members of the student body—basketball players or football players at a top-ranked Division I school can't be. No one else at school travels like those teams, no one practices like those teams, no one has that high-pressured a professional job while being a student. College is hard enough when all you have to do is study. We had to do it while also dealing with our basketball schedule—at the University of Michigan, one of the best colleges in the country. Now, you ask, would I have been able to get into the University of Michigan without ever playing basketball? Dating all the way back to junior high, if you were in my class, I probably made you think I was just fooling around. But that was a cover for the fact that I got my work done and got the grades. There was no need for everyone to know that I could handle the books. I'd rather surprise them when they didn't see it coming. I was actually in an accelerated program at Southwestern called the Pepsi School Challenge, which gave me the opportunity to meet one of my idols, Magic Johnson, when he came to the school to meet the young scholars. Nothing nerdy about that. Looking back now, I wish I had been an even more serious student in college. That would have been helpful for life after I left basketball.

All in all, it was a pretty strange duality that first year—becoming nationally known and surviving the college life—but we managed to get through it. In the sequel, things changed. Sophomore year we had the lay of the land a little more as far as academics went, so we figured out what kinds of classes we could take, how to study efficiently, what the professors were looking for. We moved off campus into our own apartments. And we became wary of the attention we received on campus at Michigan, so we started hanging more with friends we had at Eastern Michigan, which wasn't too far away.

No matter what we did, we couldn't avoid the feeling that everything that felt so right during freshman year seemed to be slipping away.

. . .

EVEN THOUGH I always felt like I was destined to be a successful NBA player—that is, rich—from the time I was ten, I definitely saw college basketball as part of the plan. Playing in March Madness and getting to the Final Four were points that I wanted to check off in my career. As a freshman, the experience delivered in every way I could have imagined. As a sophomore, my eyes started opening up to some other, less idealistic details.

It started during the summer between freshman and sophomore years when the team took a trip to Europe. We flew over for a nine-game exhibition series in several different countries. Coach Fisher figured it would be a good bonding experience for the team. I thought it was one of the worst ideas I'd ever heard. I still had the hood mentality. Why did I need to go anywhere besides Detroit? (Yup, it sounds like stupid reasoning to me now, too.) I acted about as immaturely as you could expect from someone with that attitude, and my teammates had the same approach. On our most infamous night on the trip, a few of us snuck out of our hotel for a little adventure. We knew there was a casino nearby, and figured we would be able to grow our per diem money if we found it. I'd been gambling since I was in junior high with dice and numbers games, so I steered us to the blackjack table and started doing my thing. Well, an hour later, "my thing" had cost me all my money—and everyone else had busted out, too.

The only way to get home that late at night was a cab, but none of us had any cash for the driver. This was long before credit and debit cards in taxis, and none of us had any money left at the hotel either. So we hatched a plan to jump out of the cab a few blocks from the hotel. I'd jumped out of more than a few Blue Eagle cabs in my day in Detroit. Great idea, right? Well, not so much when, first, the hotel doors were locked that late at night and, second, we'd already told the driver where we were going! The coaching staff were thrilled to be woken up for that one. Good thing we were smarter on the court than on the street.

What was most ironic about that little escapade is how young and inexperienced it makes us seem. During the rest of the trip we didn't feel like kids at all. Not with the stands full, the pro teams opposing us, and everyone getting paid in one way or another, except for us. While the hotels, the meals, and the plane ride were nice, when we got home, what had we earned? We were going back to the hood where there were no free meals, or per diem, for the rest of the summer. And where I had to get a job to make some pocket money for the school year to come. You could find jerseys and T-shirts for sale with our numbers and likenesses on them. But we never saw a penny.

The NCAA does permit players to get paid appearances at camps, but when we tried to make a couple of bucks that way, it turned out more trouble was waiting. One time that summer, Chris, Eric Riley, and I were booked, for pay, to judge a camp's slam-dunk contest. We did that, and a few other things, and then began to leave, since we'd been there for the time that had been agreed upon. Except the people who had brought us in wanted us to stay longer. We weren't guests at a party. We couldn't leave until they paid us, and they were making us stay for our money. Nowadays, I know how to handle a situation like that. Everything—from what we were doing to how we were being paid—would have been clear well before we got there. At nineteen years of age, it wasn't as smooth.

There was another problem. They wanted to pay us with checks. I didn't have a checking account. I looked at the check they gave me like it was anthrax—what was I going to do with *that*? So when we told the guy who was running the event we needed cash, it got a little contentious. Anyway, you know how it was reported: with a focus not just on our purported immaturity, but also the supposed controversy of us doing a paid appearance. (Which most people didn't know was totally legal, according to NCAA rules.)

The incident was just another reminder of how far we were from the giant adrenaline rush that had defined our freshman season. Really, it was all too predictable. Nineteen-year-olds cast in the role of big-time stars, expected to go and charm huge crowds. On the one hand, we'd been in the spotlight since the start of high school. On the other hand, we were still young and carrying the ever-bigger chip on our shoulder about money we weren't getting.

THE COURT remained our sanctuary. That was the one place where everything could still feel right. The cheers at Crisler Arena that year were as loud as ever. The boos and the taunting on the road made us actually feel at home. In the preseason poll, we were the top-ranked team in the country. No more of this upstart thing: We felt ready to go undefeated. And we were ready to make sure, just like last season, that basketball was just the beginning of the stories told about us.

Before our first game, against Rice University, Chris and I were playing video games in our hotel room when Jimmy, Ray, and one of Ray's homeboys, a guy named Little Rob, came in with some fly Nike socks that they'd just gotten at the mall. The socks were cool: gray, instead of the normal white, with the blue Nike swoosh. Ray was talking about how he was going to wear these out, and it made me think about my old high school teammate, Voshon Lenard. Voshon, to add a little style, used to wear dress socks over his white gym socks in Southwestern games. Eventually I followed him, as did a few other players on our team. It was just another way to add to our persona on the court.

I had an idea. I asked Ray and Jimmy and Little Rob if they had any black socks at that store. Black, I thought, would be a fly match with our dark-blue-and-maize uniforms. (I know—not a perfect match.) They agreed, so we paused our video game and went back to the mall to get black socks for the whole team. We could barely find any pairs of black in the whole mall. We actually found only four pairs of Nikes, which would be for Ray, Jimmy, Chris, and Juwan—and then I got a pair of black dress socks in a department store, to wear over my whites, like I used to at Southwestern.

Now we had to figure out how to actually wear them in the game that night. They call it a "uniform" for a reason. You can't just change it when you want. Our equipment manager, Bobby Bland, would never let it happen, and neither would the coaches. We hatched a plan: We would slip away in the locker room to get dressed one-by-one in bathroom stalls, then put on our warm-ups and keep the pants on in the pre-game and layup lines. At the very last minute, we'd strip down to our shorts. That's exactly what we did. The coaches were shocked, but they weren't going to stop the game and make us change our socks. Better to ask for forgiveness than permission.

Socks or not, we played sloppy in that opening game, winning by four against a Rice team that wouldn't make the NCAA Tournament. The papers and the fans took notice of our new look. What was the response? Well, think about how many black socks Nike (and Adidas, and Reebok, and Under Armour, and whoever else) has sold since that night in Houston.

Now think about how much of that money went to the kids in that hotel room in Houston who came up with the whole thing.

WE DIDN'T go undefeated. We lost to Duke, in Durham, which sucked; twice to Indiana; and also to Iowa. The conference losses pretty much cost us the Big Ten title, though not the big prize we were eyeing. Still, with a 26-4 regular-season record, there were lots of highlights. We won a holiday tournament in Hawaii, knocking off North Carolina in the semifinal, with the game-winning shot by yours truly. We beat Kansas, Purdue, Iowa State, Michigan State, and a whole bunch of other tough teams. The game that stands out for me—not just because it was a great victory, but because of everything else it represented—was Illinois. It proved the media's lack of understanding about where I came from and its desire to portray me and our team in a certain light.

Let's rewind to October, just before the season started. Like a lot of weekend mornings, I was kicking it at my boy Freddie D's house over on Cloverlawn Street in Detroit. Freddie and I had known each other since Southwestern, when he was the manager of the basketball team. His mom had died at some point, and now that high school was over, he lived alone. And like a lot of kids whose parents aren't around for whatever reason, Freddie's house had become the hangout spot, the place we could go to play video games, drink a little bit, just chill out. Hanging out on the block wasn't something I had stopped doing just because I'd become part of the Fab Five. Just because I got a scholarship didn't mean the whole neighborhood got one, too. School and the hood were separated by just a half-hour drive, and I tried to straddle both worlds. Freddie was a good dude, not into anything real bad, but you couldn't say the same thing about everyone else who came through his spot. I knew that, and for better or worse, I didn't care.

Anyway, that morning I was sitting on Freddie's couch, playing Madden with a couple of other dudes that I knew a little bit. What I didn't know is that one of them had some crack cocaine rocks in his pocket and had gotten himself mixed up with an undercover officer to sell those drugs. One minute we're playing Madden, and the next minute a team of undercover cops is banging on the door, barging into the living room, whipping out the badges and guns, securing the premises. It was pretty much what you see on TV. They came in vans, disguised as dry cleaners.

While the scene unfolded, I was defiant, laughing at the cops, talking to them, asking them incredulously what they thought they were going to find. They proceeded to go through bookshelves, knife up the couches, dump out cereal boxes, looking everywhere they could for some huge stash of drugs that wasn't there. Then, boom, they go through this one guy's pockets.

I'll never forget when the cop said, "We got rocks." What? "He's got rocks. You're all arrested." "But what's our crime?" "Loitering in a 'place where drugs were stored.'" "So what now? We going downtown?" "No. Here you go." They literally gave me a ticket. You know, the kind you get when you miss a stop sign. And that was that. We all go home.

Okay, what now? Honestly, I didn't know. I told my mom what had happened, told my friends, but my (foolish) plan was to tell no one else—thinking that no one in Ann Arbor would ever find out. I didn't want it impacting my scholarship or eligibility or anything like that.

The plan worked, for about five months. Inevitably, the story leaked out to someone, and the press investigated it. One morning in early March, I got into my green Dodge Shadow, wiped off the snow, and drove to my normal breakfast spot, Bob Evans. I opened the paper while I was waiting for my food, and—Whoa!—I'm on the front page. Jalen Rose, caught in a crack house bust. Jalen Rose, drug dealer. Jalen Rose, crackhead.

A couple of things to set straight before I wrap up how this story ended. First, that house was no crack house. I know what a crack house is—knew it then, know it now. This was a friend's house where we hung out, and a dude happened to come by who had drugs (three crummy ten-dollar rocks) in his pocket. That could have happened in the suburbs as easily as it could have happened on the block. Second, the subtle criticism associated with the coverage implicated me for hanging out in my old neighborhood. Well, where was I supposed to hang out when I wasn't at school? Today, a lot of programs build infrastructures where athletes can live year-round if they want to, to keep kids out of situations they shouldn't be in. Back then, there was no such thing. Plus, I didn't have the desire to do that anyway. My old friends were the best way I could get away to escape from the craziness of the Fab Five. I loved the mania most of the time, but quiet times back in reality can be refreshing, you know?

I got huge support from my Michigan family. I didn't get suspended, and everyone had my back the whole way. We ended up having a press conference to address the whole thing. But I wasn't going to give the media what they wanted. I let them know I didn't feel like I had done anything wrong that day, and also that this hadn't fazed me one bit. Chris came to the conference for moral support, and helped keep me calm with a bunch of *Scarface* jokes. Still, I was not happy about the whole thing. I was upset and disappointed in myself that I hadn't dealt with the situation the right way from the beginning. But I wasn't going to let anyone else, least of all the media, see that. Part of me even felt, *Hey, let them attack me, fire me up even more.*

So our next game was at Illinois, at Assembly Hall. We win the opening tip, and as the point guard, I get the ball first. The chant started immediately: "CRACK HOUSE ... CRACK HOUSE." Initially, I didn't even realize they were talking about me, until it occurred to me, who else would they be talking about? Then I get to the free throw line, and they're chanting the Nancy Reagan chant: "JUST SAY NO ... JUST SAY NO." Was I embarrassed? Yeah. But that other part of me said, *I gotta embrace this. I gotta be a dogg about it. My teammates are here with me, we're playing together— that's all that matters.*

After a while, I started putting my hand to my ear during their chants, like Hulk Hogan, egging them on as if I couldn't hear them. It only made them get louder, which was perfect, because it stoked my adrenaline higher. My teammates sensed that. They were watching out for me, staying close to me on the bench during timeouts, making sure I knew I had their support, and feeding me the ball every chance they could get. It was close all the way, and then, when we were down in the closing seconds, I hit a shot to tie it, and then got a steal to force overtime. In OT, I couldn't be stopped, putting on the finishing touches.

I played all forty-five minutes. Twenty-three points. Eight rebounds. At the end I put one index finger to my lips, letting the crowd know when it was time to quiet down.

Take that to your crack house.

SMALL SIDE note before I get to the tournament.

We were college boys, and we were famous.

The Fab Five did okay with the women.

Enough said.

SOPHOMORE YEAR actually should have felt more familiar to me. We were the favorites. As freshmen, we weren't expected to win, something I wasn't accustomed to. That had made us an easy team to root for if you were young, understood what we were about, and liked being part of the oldest story in sports: the underdog.

In the sequel, we were the Big Bad Wolf. The team that was easy to hate. We thrived off that energy, though when things like the "crack house" incident arose, it could be a reminder of just how intense it all was, for the fans and for us. During our game against Michigan State, in East Lansing in February, the chants were real bad. The n-word was flying at us, and that was just from the uncreative fans. We ended up winning the game, and even though Michigan State sucked that year, considering the rivalry, it was a great win. We decided to celebrate in front of fans by rubbing it in—literally. A few of us sat down on the Spartan *S* near midcourt after the final buzzer, and—how's this for classy—rubbed our butts on the floor.

It's easy to look back twenty years later, shake your head, and call us immature. Argue that we should have walked off the court, not try and incite a riot. But that would be ignoring the reality of our situation. The fact is, we had accomplished the most important mission in our lives that week: beating our archrival. To do that we had to get ourselves into a mental state in which every fiber of our bodies, minds, and hearts was devoted to that task. That meant getting hyped, that meant a lot of shouting and trash-talk, that meant—to paraphrase one of my favorite athletes of all time, Lawrence Taylor—"goin' out there like a bunch of crazed dogs and havin' some fun." There are going to be consequences to that once the final whistle blows.

The only thing I regret about that particular stunt is that I forgot that from center court we still had to walk to our locker room. And on that short walk, the fans got us good. They threw change at us, water bottles, food, and showered us with beer and soda. And then, when we were leaving, they tried to tip over our bus.

They couldn't. We drove back to Ann Arbor with the win.

A LITTLE bit of spice in the Michigan–Michigan State rivalry—a little bit of beer throwing and bus tipping—wasn't particularly distinctive to the Fab Five. What was unique was something else that rained down on us: hypocrisy.

It started right at Michigan. The so-called distinguished alumni started calling in, writing letters to Coach Fisher and the administration, complaining that the way we conducted ourselves wasn't be-fitting of "Michigan Men." These, of course, were the same alumni who would have fired Coach, and his entire staff, if they hadn't successfully recruited us. And the same alumni whose university was suddenly back in the national spotlight thanks to us, which had invaluable benefits for the school as a whole. I'd also venture to guess that as often as they were shaking their heads about us at their country clubs and inside their law firms, they were also sneak-ing off into their dens and family rooms on weekends, putting on their Michigan hats and shirts, and screaming just as loudly as we did when the refs screwed us out of a call.

Then there was the hypocrisy everywhere else. Maybe the epi-sode that sums it up best is what Bill Walton told Roy Firestone on *Up Close,* the old interview show preceding *SportsCenter* on ESPN. I remember watching the show in my apartment, just before the tour-nament, sophomore year. He called us "one of the most overrated and underachieving teams of all time," "guys who epitomize what is wrong with a lot of basketball players," which apparently was that "they think they're better than they are. They don't come out to win games. They come out defending something they don't have." (I guess he was referring to a national title there.) He continued: "They come along, they cruise, they come in and say, 'We're Michigan, we're really great because everybody says we're great.'"

Now, that was a long time ago. I've gotten to know Bill Walton pretty well since then, and I have become a big fan and a good friend of his. He's always frank and candid, and will always be one of the best college players of all time. But let's talk for a second about where Bill was coming from. The UCLA tradition. The leg-endary John Wooden, who apparently did everything perfectly and was a model of what college sports aspired to be, even if when you sniff around the history of that program, you find out that there may have been a few envelopes being handed around to a few players during his era.

So while we're at it, how about a few quotes some UCLA fans might be familiar with?

"Failure is not fatal, but a failure to change might be."

"You can't let praise or criticism get to you. It's a weakness to get caught up in either one."

"Be true to yourself."

I don't know about you, but to me, all those quotes sound like they could be about the Fab Five.

Every one of them was uttered by John Wooden himself.

Oh, one more quote. This one from Walton again. His thoughts on how we'd do in the 1993 NCAA Tournament.

"This is a team I don't think is doing well and won't do well in the tournament."

Oh, is that right?

WE GOT the top seed in the West, which meant we'd start our journey back to the summit in Arizona. We beat Coastal Carolina by thirty, but then got a wake-up call against who else, Bill Walton's alma mater, UCLA, in the second round, going down by nineteen in the first half to a school that would win the national title two years later. Nut check. We came all the way back, got through some hairy moments to get it to overtime, and then Jimmy tipped in a miss off one of my shots to win it. Consider us woken up. We got past George Washington, led by the late Yinka Dare, and then met the team we'd played at the beginning of our freshman run, John Chaney's Temple Owls. Chaney had come to my house in Detroit to try and recruit me in high school. His teams played a familiar brand of basketball, tough and unforgiving. They were as strong a team as any we played in that era, and that game was like being back in west Detroit. They had a forward named William Cunningham who spent the whole game just trying to punk Chris. But we fought and fought, and found a way to win. We were going to our second straight Final Four.

It was hardly a flawless tournament run—but look back at the history of March Madness, and you'll see how many Final Four teams barely get through most of their games. It becomes as much about guts as skills, as much about staying together as playing great. Your goal should be to peak when you get to the Final Four. Which, after shaking Temple in the last ten minutes of the game, is what we were doing.

Finally, the sequel was feeling right again. We knew Chris was probably going to do something very, very few players did back then—turn pro as a sophomore after the season ended. We knew the stakes as we went to one of the party capitals of the United States, New Orleans. The media frenzy was nothing new. The hype was nothing new. Duke was long gone—Jason Kidd and Lamond Murray at Cal had upset them in the second round. We had Kentucky in front of us, and then the winner of North Carolina–Kansas. Three of the most storied programs in the history of college basketball, and the Fab Five.

The day before our game against Kentucky, we got off the practice floor and Mitch Albom, the *Detroit Free Press* columnist who'd been working on a book about us, came up to me. Mitch and I had known each other a little bit back in high school, and for the book, he'd already been talking to me, my mom, and a bunch of other people. Just another guy making a dollar off the Fab Five, even if it was cool having a book being written about us.

As we walked to the locker room, Mitch handed me an envelope with a letter inside.

What's this? I asked him.

It's a letter from your dad.

6. The Inside Story of One of the Most Famous Plays in Basketball History

It's a funny thing about time, and life. Even if you're lucky and you're around for eighty, ninety years, everything comes down to things that happened in one day, or a few hours, or even just a couple of seconds. A job interview, a first date, some stroke of luck or fate that changed everything. Sports amplify that reality. You could do everything right 99.9 percent of your career, but if you can't get it done in that 0.1 percent, then that's what people remember, and that's what defines your legacy.

On the one hand, it's unfair. So much of what happens in that 0.1 percent of the time is out of your control. On the other hand, those instances aren't isolated moments of time; they are part of everything else. Not just how much you've practiced, and how much you've prepared, but what you've gone through—experiences, adversity, successes, and failures. All set you up for those handful of moments that, for better or worse, matter more than all the others.

People still come up to me to talk about the Fab Five. They tell me how they remember our games, and how they appreciate all the ways we impacted basketball, and everything around it. Once in a while, though, usually when I'm at a bar or a restaurant, when someone's had a few drinks, they bring up the Timeout. They tell me where they were when they watched that title game in '93, what they remember, how they couldn't believe it. It comes up, and all of us—Jimmy, Ray, Juwan, myself, and of course Chris—have to live with it. Because no matter who called the timeout, and why he did it, for the Fab Five that moment was about all of us. We can't detach it from everything that had happened in the 99.9 percent of the rest of the time. We walked into the Superdome that night in New Orleans as brothers, and we walked out as brothers.

That will never change.

Despite what may have happened since.

Despite why it happened at all.

OVERALL, I'M a big fan of Mitch Albom. He's a great writer, and he's done great things for Detroit, including a ton of charity work headlined by his organization, S.A.Y. Detroit, which helps out the city's neediest people in many ways. Mitch has had a lot of success in his career. He's even had a bit of controversy. But I'm not sure anyone has given much thought to the fact that in 1993, he took it upon himself to seek out the father I hadn't had any contact with in twenty years. Then, on the eve of one of the biggest games of my career, to hand me that letter with no warning. I understand, now more than ever, that it's the media's job to sell papers and magazines. Still, looking back, taking it upon himself to create a story that he could use for his book crossed a line.

Typically on the college level, the sports information office is supposed to protect players from the media when necessary. But by that point in time, late in our sophomore year, the athletic department viewed Mitch's book as their book, because the program, and the university, were going to benefit from an exclusive inside look at our team. It was essentially free publicity, for recruits, for prospective students, and for alumni donors. They gave him access to us anytime he wanted. Now, forget about the fact that the five of us weren't going to see a dime of the book money—thanks to Albom's intrepid reporting, the school had put our team at risk by allowing a writer to possibly mess with the head of one of its star players right before the Final Four.

I'm not bringing this up to make any excuses. I will say right here that Mitch had nothing to do with the result of the games, and nothing to do with how I played. I've never spoken to him about this, and it would be interesting to hear what he thinks of the whole episode now. And also, since he got paid twice—once for his job as a reporter, and then for writing the book (keep getting dem checks, Mitch!)—maybe we could talk it over and he could make a donation to JRLA to clear this all up. Mitch, you know where to find me!

Anyway, back to New Orleans. Mitch hands me this letter from Jimmy Walker, and a phone number if I wanted to call him. I asked him where Walker was living. Atlanta, he said. Mitch asked me a few more questions, trying to draw a reaction and to get me to reveal my emotions at that moment. I wasn't going to give him much of a story. Never let them see you sweat. Always stay in control. Street rules.

Back in my hotel room, I came close to calling my father. I really did. But I didn't. I had been dealing with distractions my entire life.

I wasn't about to let this one suddenly ruin everything. Learning who my father was in that basement at St. Cecilia's had basically defined my outlook on what my destiny was. But that didn't mean the man himself had any place in the story of where I'd ended up.

I put the letter in my bag, the envelope still sealed. There was no good reason to open it, at least right then. The most important fact had already been made clear.

My father knew my name.

THERE WERE three number one seeds and a number two in the Final Four that year. Kentucky was favored over us by seven points. Rick Pitino had taken over the program in the late '80s after it had NCAA trouble, and had rebuilt it into a high-flying, up-tempo monster that had been blowing opponents out all season long. They'd won each of their tournament games by at least twenty-one points, while we'd barely snuck by in three of our four victories. They had Jamal Mashburn, who would go on to be a lottery pick just a few spots behind Chris in the upcoming draft, and Travis Ford, Dale Brown, and Tony Delk, all great college players, too. There was only one way to beat them: slow the game down, and be patient and confident in one another to work for the best shot.

There's one other key to the Final Four: remembering that March Madness isn't made for teams who dominate. Being able to handle yourself in the midst of all that late-game pressure has always been what's most important. No matter how experienced you are, no matter how many battles you've won over the course of the season, you almost want to be in that desperation mode, or at least familiar with it, all throughout the tournament. Coasting is easy, but the longer your run goes on, the more dangerous it gets.

Everyone thought Kentucky was going to roll over us. Which was perfect. It made us the underdog, and gave us something to shoot for. Everyone in basketball thinks the Wildcats are going to win? Outstanding. Everyone in the country thinks these punks are finally gonna get their asses handed to them by one of the most storied college basketball programs in the country? Perfect. A couple of Detroit rappers named Kaos and Maestro actually wrote a song about us beating Kentucky, to pump us up. Not that we needed any extra motivation.

Sure enough, when Kentucky came out expecting to blow us out of the gym in the opening minutes, we stood our ground and took an early lead. Immediately they were completely out of sorts. They hadn't played a challenging game in almost a month. We went into halftime with a five-point lead, making it double digits early in the second. Beating them took relentless defense, and you know the referees never loved us. So while Jimmy kept Travis Ford from hitting any threes, he also fouled out late in the second half. Kentucky was able to come back to tie it, and to send us into overtime again. Nothing new for us. Just another nut check. Their best player, Mashburn, after scoring twenty-six points (one fewer than Chris), fouled out himself early in OT, and they were pretty much done after that. We won by three, 81–78.

Were we talking trash the whole way? You bet.

Were we playing a brand of team basketball we didn't get credit for? Absolutely.

And our second straight national title game was forty-eight hours away.

IN '92, Duke had been the better team. The competition bore that out clearly, both in the game we played them at the beginning of the season, with nothing to lose, and in the title game, when there was a national championship at stake. North Carolina in the '93 title game was a different story. We should have beaten them. We beat them in Hawaii in the holiday tournament, and that was with Ray injured. The Tar Heels were a great college team, with stars like George Lynch and Eric Montross and a great coach in Dean Smith. But we were still better. I think we could have beaten them that year nine out of ten times. I really do. But that's the beauty of the NCAA Tournament. In a seven-game series, the better team almost always wins. In one game, anything can happen.

It's interesting to look back from the analyst's perspective now, and try and break down what went wrong in the most famous game I ever played in. Did we feel like we had slain the dragon in Kentucky, and that let the air out of our balloon a little bit? Yeah, maybe. Did we feel like we had silenced a lot of doubters by repeating what they said was a fluke, getting to the title game the year before? It's a possibility. Were we too confident? No way. We went into *every* game bursting with confidence and swagger. It was one of our biggest weapons.

Whatever the reason, during the game we were just . . . a little off. Donald Williams went wild that night, scoring twenty-five points. He torched everyone who guarded him. I scored twelve points but didn't get to the free throw line. In fact, we took just seven free throws all game. We were down six at halftime, and trailed most of the second half as well. Even when we were able to take a lead, we'd give it up quickly. Fans know the feeling when they're watching their team play and it just doesn't feel right, regardless of what the scoreboard says. The players can have the same feeling. It's like when you just can't get comfortable in a pair of shoes. On the court, there's no way to go back into the closet and change into something else.

The one guy who kept us in the game was Chris. Go back and watch the game, and you'll see him single-handedly keeping us alive in the second half, with rebounds, putbacks, dunks, you name it. It must have felt like playing for Detroit Country Day for him, being the one guy in the middle who had to do everything. He was just as dominant against the North Carolina Tar Heels as he was against some private school in Grosse Pointe, Michigan. They could not stop him.

We had to burn a timeout late in the second half, when Juwan couldn't get an inbounds pass in off the press. That meant, with a little less than a minute to go, after Ray nailed a long two-pointer to get us back within three points, the timeout we called was our last. And in the huddle, it was reiterated by the coaches, the trainers, the other players. We had no more timeouts. That was clear to all of us.

We turned up the pressure on defense, and they turned the ball over. Then Chris got a putback on a three-pointer I missed, getting us to one point down, and we fouled with twenty seconds left. They hit the first free throw and missed the second, and Chris got the rebound. We've got the ball, down two, twenty seconds to go.

At this point, we've played together long enough that we all know what we normally do in this situation, exactly what Coach outlined for us in the huddle just prior. Chris will get the rebound off a miss, outlet to me, I'll take it up, try and get a three-pointer off a pick-and-roll, or, if they bottle that up, then I swing it to Chris to probably take a shot. If his man shows, then that gives him an opportunity to swing it to Jimmy or Rob Pelinka, who were in the corners. That's our play.

That didn't happen.

Chris hesitated a bit after the miss, and by the time he looked up to me, George Lynch had doubled back into the passing lane. Chris was halfway into passing it to me when he realized this, so he traveled, taking a step forward an instant before he started his dribble. The ref, right on top of the play, somehow didn't call it. I remember this thought going through my head: *Man, he just traveled . . . they didn't call it . . . that's our break . . . we're gonna win this thing.* Next, Chris decides to take the ball up himself. This didn't mess us up one bit. In fact, Chris was probably the only power forward in the country—college or pro—who could be trusted to handle the ball in that situation. This wasn't some gump forward with no business dribbling. This was someone who ran the break for us a lot of times and was capable of starting a lot of great plays. Really, one of the best passing big men the game has ever seen. But instead of going straight up the floor, he started veering toward our bench. And I remember wondering why my man, Derrick Phelps, and Chris's man, Lynch, were still double-teaming him. Honestly, it was almost like *they* forgot we didn't have a timeout left, and were trying to trap Chris and force him to call it. So I became a trailer in the play, like any fast break, going to the elbow area or the three-point area, and waiting for an open shot off a double-team on Chris. I had already calculated that if I didn't have the shot, I could just take it to the basket. Our other three guys on the floor were surely thinking the same kind of thoughts. Your job on the basketball court is to always be prepared for what you're going to do next, whether the ball is coming to you or not.

I wasn't thinking that Chris would try and call a timeout. But he did.

Need I tell you the rest? With eleven seconds left, the timeout violation meant Carolina got two free throws and the ball. We'd had the chance to tie the game, or even win it, right in front of us. But now the game was all but over.

My initial reaction, in the moment, was pretty much total denial. It had to be, considering my mindset: that despite how badly we'd played, despite the fact that the game never felt quite right, somehow we were still going to win that game. So in the huddle right after that, after Carolina called their own timeout, I remember being upset at anyone who was hanging their head, anyone who didn't believe that we could still win the game. But when the final buzzer sounded, there was nothing we could do about it: We'd lost the game we were meant to win.

THE REALIZATION always kind of settles in gradually, amid the frantic scene of any postgame. In a national title game, with people running all over the court, and the other team celebrating, it's more surreal than any game anyone plays all year. With Duke, it started to sink in with five minutes to go, maybe even more. So it wasn't as dramatic; we had time to prepare for it. Here we went from having a chance to win the game to being finished in eleven seconds.

The first thing I did was to go to Coach Fisher, who a lot of people had criticized for not "disciplining" us the way he should have the past two years. But he'd believed in us, and so as we walked off the floor, I put my arm around Coach, told him that I loved him, and promised him that I was going to get him back to this point again and win him a title.

When we got into the locker room, Chris was already there, lying facedown on the carpet. Head completely down. Bruce Madej, our sports information director, came up to me and said, I need you to find a way to help me get this kid up, because there's no way I can send him into the press conference looking like this. So the other guys and I, we got him together, got him to the media, and Juwan, Jimmy, and Coach Fisher did their interviews with him, together, as a team. I stayed in the locker room—if I didn't have to, I didn't want to be in a situation where I might say something I'd regret. Afterwards, we hustled Chris out to the team bus, and his mom came on the bus. He sat next to her and, honestly, he cried the whole way back to the hotel. Sobbed. It was the only sound anyone made that whole ride.

The dynamic of the whole situation actually made it easier for me to deal with the loss, because I was so focused on looking after one of my closest friends in the world, who I'd been playing ball with since we were twelve, and who had made probably the worst decision he's ever made on the basketball court in front of the biggest audience ever to watch him play. That took the attention off my sadness. Though what's interesting is I remember starting to feel some guilt of my own, too. What could I have done differently? Should I have gone and gotten the basketball right after the rebound? Or maybe just followed him into the corner? Everyone has regrets when something rotten like that happens, thoughts of saving the day like Superman, even if they're ridiculous. But those were the kinds of thoughts running through my brain at that time.

We got back to the hotel and had to hustle through the back entrance of the lobby up to our rooms to avoid the craziness there, getting scrambled apart in the process. But upstairs, we all got together again, sitting in one of the rooms—on the beds, the floor, the chairs—still processing what the hell had just happened.

THE PROBLEM with one instant like the Timeout defining your legacy is that it's impossible to ever put your finger truly on its cause. What does it really mean, anyway? When that game ended, Chris was still the best basketball player on the floor, for either team. He was still the best college basketball player in the country. So how did one bad decision change him as a player? Was it really some sort of window into who he really was as a player? I mean, how many other times, in the heat of battle, in crunch time in so many other games, did Chris come through? So was thirty-five million people watching in the final really that different from, say, a few million watching when he made big plays in other tournament games? That's the problem with the way sports are analyzed. There's no middle ground. He's either the guy who makes the big play or the guy who blows it.

But twenty-some years later, look what's happened: It's my job to be one of those analysts. To tell you why something took place, even if most of the time there's no definitive answer. On the one hand, there's the explanation of the heat of the moment. Chris was in the corner, near our bench, and it's pretty clear from the video (as you can see in our documentary) that there were some guys on the bench who were screaming at him to call timeout. Guys who hadn't played all game, who hadn't been listening in the huddle when the coaching staff reminded us we had no timeouts. Whether or not Chris heard the coaches, when you're in the corner, getting trapped by Derrick Phelps and George Lynch, and your teammates are yelling at you, the peer pressure can be pretty convincing.

Going big picture: Can a player like Chris Webber be both an incredibly talented superstar and a player who, in a moment of maximum adversity, chokes? Can both those attributes and descriptions be in his basketball DNA? The answer is, Absolutely.

And to me, his identity is further defined by the fact that he's never come out and really talked about it in the twenty-plus years since. Since he doesn't own it, he'll never get over it.

The impact of that fact, as much as the timeout itself, has tarnished the legacy of the Fab Five.

UP IN that hotel room, we talked about the play. What had happened, what could have been different, all that. We were dealing with our own devastation, but there was also the reality of how many other people had been rooting for our downfall and got to see it in brutal fashion. We wanted to silence the haters, the naysayers, the critics. Instead, we gave them an opportunity to celebrate our misfortune. That started to get the blood flowing a little bit. Hey, this loss was just another reason for them to hate on the Fab Five, which they were going to do anyway.

Then we moved on to everything else that awaited us, particularly Chris, regardless of what just happened. To me it was clear he should leave school after that season. He was set to be the number one pick, to make millions of dollars. Winning a national championship had been our goal from the outset, but in this sophomore sequel we'd learned that life was only going to get more complicated. It wasn't worth Chris staying to live through that again.

At that moment, the writers were typing away at their computers, writing stories about how the Fab Five were a failure, how we'd blown it again, how we had it coming to us. But in that hotel room, we were the same guys we'd been that afternoon, before the game had taken place. Losing the game didn't make us losers. It signaled the fact that we sucked during that game. It meant we were the losers of *that* game. But there were a lot more victories available to us in life. I understood that then, and I understand that now. We thought, *Okay, Chris, you made a terrible mistake, a dumb-ass mistake. You know it, we know it. But we're still brothers. What else is up?*

We got dressed, and headed out as the Fab Five one more time. Bourbon Street wasn't far away, and it was packed. Some people high-fived us, and some people screamed at us. We took it in stride. We found our way to the club with the longest line, walked to the front, the bouncers lifted the velvet rope, and we strolled in.

The last thing I remember that night is looking back over my shoulder. The Carolina players were standing there, still waiting in line.

7. What Didn't Happen and What Really Happened

You realize everything I just wrote about never happened, right?

I'm serious. Search NCAA record books, and try to find an official account of our sophomore year, our second straight run to the Final Four, the Timeout Game. You'll find nothing. Just a big blank space for that whole season. Which makes no sense. If you were alive in 1992 and 1993, and a sports fan, you remember what happened, and you'll never forget it.

The funny thing is, that actually almost makes too much sense. In our sports culture, an organization like the National Collegiate Athletic Association can decide to erase certain parts of history, while expressing no interest in giving back the billions of dollars it made off that history, and off the young men who were at the center of it.

As great as college basketball will always be, it has long been so great in spite of, not because of, the NCAA. Though just because it's a terrible organization doesn't mean that the problems it faces are easy to solve. The NCAA just so happens to do a particularly poor, shameless job of approaching its problems. College sports, with regard to Division I football and basketball, is really a square peg stuck in a round hole. This idea of amateur sports taking place within the confines of a multibillion-dollar business is ludicrous. Those two things don't go together naturally. I understand universities have to make money. I understand shoe companies have to make money. I understand television networks have to make money. What I don't understand is why the young athletes who are making every last cent of it possible can't be entitled to any money in return.

As I write this, college sports is in what may be the early stages of a revolution. Lawsuits, a redistribution of power to the Big Five conferences, playoffs in football—all these things are changing the system. I have a few simple ideas of my own on some changes that could make things better. But first let me explain how I ended up in the middle of history that somehow disappeared into thin air.

WE WERE never under investigation while we were at school. It all didn't heat up until the cold of a Detroit winter, February 1996, three years after our second championship game appearance. By then, the Fab Five were all out of Michigan—I was playing in Denver with the Nuggets, and Chris and Juwan were together on the Washington Bullets. Meanwhile, Mateen Cleaves, a high school All-American from Flint, was being recruited by Michigan (Mateen—not only did you go on to win a title for State, but you set off this chain reaction!) and was on his official recruiting visit. Cleaves was coming back from a party with a bunch of Wolverine players—including Maurice Taylor, the driver, and the late Robert "Tractor" Traylor—when their car crashed. A Ford Explorer, to be specific. After the accident, when people started wondering how Maurice Taylor could own such a nice car, the trail led back to Ed

Martin. Yes, the same Ed Martin who I'd first met during boot camp at Southwestern bringing those Chicken Littles to practice, and who I, like so many other young basketball players in Detroit, had gotten to know so well, and to appreciate so much.

The backstory of that night in 1996 is that the players were going from Ann Arbor to a party in Detroit and had stopped by Ed's house; Ed gave them some money, and then they unfortunately had the accident (which broke Tractor's arm and cost him the rest of the season).

Now, the NCAA report that later came out would like you to believe that Ed had a bunch of envelopes stuffed with hundreds on the table, and everyone got an envelope, and then got their pick of automobiles. And there were also rumors that Ed was actually hosting a party, and there were strippers and drugs there that he provided, even if no one had ever made an allegation of that nature about Ed before, or after. Eventually, after "sources" threw some tales like that against the wall, the raised eyebrows focused on the money, and the car, and the status of Ed Martin at the University of Michigan. But the fact is that the history of Ed Martin and these kids went far back before college. Tractor Traylor grew up in Detroit, just like I did. So did Mo Taylor. (Neither of them went to Southwestern.) Mateen Cleaves grew up in Flint. They all knew Uncle Ed like I did; all met him the same way, as young kids playing basketball. And they all lived in circumstances where they sometimes didn't have a new coat for winter, didn't have new shoes for the new season, didn't have any pocket money to spend on a Saturday night. Ed was the guy who gave it to them. Because he wanted to help them. Because he could help them. That wasn't going to change when they got to college.

I know it certainly didn't change for me. Ed gave me money

throughout my time at Michigan. Fifty dollars here, a hundred dollars there, two hundred dollars there. All in all throughout my three years at Michigan, he probably gave me a couple of thousand dollars. I borrowed his car, too, plenty of times. Why wouldn't I borrow the car if he offered? Don't you think I'd rather use a nice shiny car on a date or to a party than my beat-up Dodge Shadow? I was a college kid, and for all college kids "meal money" means money to go out on Saturday nights. Meanwhile, Ed was also still very involved in Detroit high school basketball, with all the kids I just mentioned and dozens of others who you've never heard of. Nothing changed for him either.

The Big Ten and Michigan put together an investigation soon after the crash and found only minor violations. In plain English, that means no one had done anything wrong except break a few NCAA laws, which were misguided anyway. That didn't stop the powers that be from wanting to show the public that they had done their due diligence in this supposed "shady situation." They fired Coach Fisher because of his connections to Ed. Connections? Really, Coach got fired because he kept an eye on Ed and what he was doing for the kids and occasionally stepped in when Ed committed what the NCAA might see as a violation, like buying plane tickets for players' parents to go to the tournament and watch their kids in person. Because Coach didn't report all these so-called violations, he was charged with bucking the system. In a sad way, it was fitting. For years, Coach Fisher had straddled a line few other people could: operating within the confines of a silly system of rules while also understanding where his players came from; respecting us, while also disciplining us; giving us enough leeway to play the way we did while also setting limits we knew we could not cross. But being in the middle is never easy, and eventually Coach got screwed by it.

Still, the casualties weren't close to complete. A few years later, the FBI came knocking, charging Ed in an investigation into a numbers racket at a Ford plant. The key charge was that he "laundered" the money he earned from running the numbers ring by giving it to basketball players. Basically, his money traveled the way money travels on the block: as straight cash. That's how I ended up in front of a grand jury in the spring of 2000. The government knew I was one of the kids who knew Ed best, so I must have ended up with a lot of that money. I told them what I just told you—the truth. Yeah, Ed gave me some money, but not a lot and nothing more than what he gave me in high school.

Meanwhile, the government's involvement sprang the NCAA back into action. They started a new investigation that turned up all kinds of new details, headlined by supposed five- and six-figure sums of money that Ed had given some players and their families, most prominently C-Webb. And that's when things got really ugly.

First, it got ugly for Michigan, which decided to self-impose penalties in addition to the ones coming down from the NCAA. Those penalties included basically forfeiting our entire sophomore season, when Chris was allegedly receiving money from Ed, and our Final Fours, along with some other seasons after we left, when the next generation of Michigan stars—like Taylor and Traylor—were also allegedly getting paid by Ed. With the NCAA bearing down, Michigan basically gave in and did everything for them. That's how we disappeared from the history books.

It also got ugly for Chris personally, because when testifying to the grand jury like I did, he told them he never received any money (or at least not very much money) from Ed, which contradicted other testimony. Chris was charged with lying under oath.

So that's the quick summary of it in plain language. There's a lot of stuff I glossed over. Like how every report ever written about the whole thing always notes that when the FBI came to Ed's house, he had $20,000 in cash there—"and a loaded gun." As if he were some kind of gangster, when millions of people across America (including millions that don't live in the hood) also have loaded guns in their houses. Let me ask you: If he were white, would that have been part of the story? And the $20,000 may sound shady, but it's also a "necessary evil" of doing business in the hood. It's a cash world. Again, the hood mentality doesn't translate well on the outside.

And here's something more central that I don't want to gloss over: How come Chris supposedly got $280,000 (that's the number in the NCAA's final report) from Ed and he was still driving a blue Corsica all through college? How come Chris and I were still saving our pizza cards from Thano's, which you could use to get free pizza in the school dining halls, every week? How come the two warm-up suits we got from the team were the newest things in our closet? How come Mitch Albom was following us around for an entire season, and nothing about Ed Martin is mentioned in his book? And one more: How come I was never offered that kind of money? Chris and I were 1-2 in high school, we were 1-2 (along with Juwan) in college. Ed knew us both from the time we were kids. How come he didn't give me anywhere in the stratosphere of what he supposedly gave Chris? We were both headed to the pros, both set to make millions of dollars, right?

Look, here's the truth of what happened. In April 1993, when

Chris declared for the NBA Draft, he basically held in his hand a lottery ticket—a rookie deal that would be worth almost $75 million. Of course, he would have to wait until October to start cashing the checks—even though immediately starting that April, he had to start living like a pro, getting his own place, getting a trainer, looking around for business managers, all without any money yet. Well, Ed could help, and then the idea was that Chris could pay Ed back as soon as he got his signing bonus. So Ed served as a bridge for Chris so that he didn't have to reach out to agents or to boosters. That's all.

Michigan was never going to acknowledge or make an exception for that scenario in their report. And to the NCAA, Ed was a "representative of the athletic interests of the University of Michigan." Not someone who had a "preexisting relationship," their term for someone ... exactly like him. A man who had known Chris for years (and had grown close with Chris's father), and who had no true allegiance to any institution, or anyone besides Chris. The fact is that Ed would have been behind Chris (and me, and anyone else he helped out in high school) anywhere we went to college. But somehow the officials behind the investigation came to a different sort of conclusion.

So what did the school do? It basically did what refs do when they don't have an answer—it called the equivalent of a double foul. Chris was forced to disassociate with the university for ten years, our games and records were wiped out officially, Steve Fisher lost his job, and Michigan gave itself additional sanctions. Everyone gets penalized; let's move on. The only problem is, in a basketball game, everyone does move on. In this situation, our banners, and our legacy, got buried in a box in a basement.

. . .

LET ME ask you a question: If we had grown up in the suburbs and Ed were one of our dads, or our uncles, would any of this have been an issue? And I'll say it again: If everyone involved were white, would they have ever reported that Ed had a loaded gun in his house as if he were some sort of threat?

Ed was a guy who used to take Chris and me to ACT class— made us go. Not get us drugs! He was the guy who brought food everywhere he went—seafood pizza, Chicken Littles, pies, cakes. Not guns! Ed Martin was a good man with a positive outlook, a big smile, and a wonderful family that included his wife, Hilda, and his sons, Carl and Bruce. To me, the measure of a man is how he treats people who can't do anything for him. Ninety-five percent of the kids he helped were never going to be able to pay him back or reciprocate. No one wants to write about that. No one wants to write about the coats and sneakers he bought for kids who he knew were never going to play college ball, forget about the NBA.

Why can't it be okay for a player like me to know someone with a little bit of money? Why can't it be all right for that person to send me a few hundred dollars, or hook me up with their car once in a while, when I'm in college, trying to do the right thing? Because I'm a basketball player? Because I'm black, and from the hood?

Try this: Picture your favorite college basketball player. Now picture his mom or dad or uncle or godfather giving him some spending money, or a new Jeep. What's the difference between that and Ed Martin? I didn't have a father to help support me. Neither did most of the other players. We took whatever help we could get. In the eyes of the public and the NCAA, there was no gray area. We were either model students or thugs. They decided the latter.

I'm proud to make this clear right now: Ed Martin *did* have a huge impact on the Fab Five. I'm not talking about pocket money or borrowed cars. I'm talking about the fact that he helped inspire the Fab Five to begin with. Ed was someone who made me care about Detroit, and community, and people. He taught me about real charity, the kind that makes it to the block as opposed to the kind that's about photo ops and good press. That example, from Ed, from Perry, and from others absolutely influenced my decision to stay close to home at Michigan. And to team up with Chris, and three other guys, to shock the world *together.*

That's the real heart of the hood mentality. If you grow up with money and means, you can never truly understand what it's like to be without money and means. You can never really appreciate how hard it is to, first, simply survive and support yourself and your family in the hood and, second, somehow pull yourself out. That's fine. It's nobody's fault—until people start imposing rules and expectations and norms that exist in the rest of the world, on the hood.

People think of the hood as a place where people get shot, where they get robbed, where they get beat up. And, yes, that happens there much more than other places, because people in the hood are desperate. When people are desperate, they can be driven to do some bad things. But in the hood, you'll also find people lifting each other up. Neighbors who look out for one another. People who find ways to not just survive, but thrive.

I'll tell you what bothers me most about the whole thing. You know I've never minded the haters. I practically recruited the haters in college. But the one place I don't need any hate is on the legacy of the Fab Five. Hate on the long shorts, the black socks, the bald heads, the earrings, the tattoos. That is all fine. But it's upsetting to me that the final chapter of our saga is about violations and scandal, about our Final Four run getting erased and our banners being taken down. It's upsetting to me that people think it was all a scam, that we were paid to play, and we didn't really go to college. I hear the jokes and the comments all the time. The truth is that I had to save money to fill up my car every winter I was in Ann Arbor. The truth is, we played our hearts out because we wanted to.

But the truth has nothing to do with what people want to believe.

And as far as the NCAA is concerned, the truth has no place in history.

I GLOSSED over something that I want to use to illustrate the problems of misconceptions and assumptions. When I came to Michigan in 1991, after graduating from Southwestern, Perry Watson, my high school coach, also came to Michigan as an assistant coach on Steve Fisher's staff. There was nothing illegal about that, and no one ever really made much of a fuss about this specifically, other than to raise an eyebrow or two—but honestly, that raised eyebrow is what I'm concerned with. If you read stories about the Fab Five, writers use a certain tone when talking about Perry to imply that he was some sort of slickster who had an operation going. That's complete bull.

The truth is important. Yes, Perry took a job and, yes, it was a tremendous asset to have a trusted mentor there as a guide during freshman year. He also knew Chris, and became a mentor to my other teammates. It was good for the coaching staff to have someone who their star recruits would instantly trust, and be able to communicate with.

That doesn't mean it was shady.

Perry was the coach of the best high school team in the country, a team that had been to nine straight Michigan state title games and had won two consecutive titles. Do you know what happens to high school coaches like that? They get college jobs. It's the next step up the ladder. Perry got lots of offers to leave Southwestern for college jobs before 1991. It wasn't like Michigan was doing him a favor by giving him a job.

For Perry it made sense, too. After nine straight state title games, and two straight state titles, he had pretty much proved he was the best. A new opportunity sounded enticing. Furthermore, the job led Perry to a place where he could make a larger impact on young people in Detroit than he was making at Southwestern. Perry stayed two years at Michigan and then left (before me) to take the head coaching job at the University of Detroit (now Detroit Mercy). That job gave him an opportunity to take his mission to a bigger stage. He could encourage the best players in the city to come to college and play for him while making a difference at the college in a number of ways. He spent fifteen years at Detroit, taking his teams to two NCAA tournaments and producing star players like Willie Green and Jermaine Jackson. He was the first guy to make that program relevant since Dick Vitale coached there in the 1970s. Perry retired a few years back, when, as I said earlier, the recruiting game changed too much, and he just found it too hard—too depressing, really—to reach the local kids he wanted to help. (Now he actually does some scouting for the Orlando Magic.)

Are there programs out there that give jobs to people associated with certain players as part of wink-wink recruiting packages? Yes, absolutely. It happens all the time. But let me ask you this: When a company hires an important new employee to run a division, doesn't that employee often bring along a colleague they trust? Isn't that understood as a smart thing to do? Of course, in college sports, as in any business, at times an associate, or a family member even, gets a no-show job or a position that's beyond the pale of what's acceptable. But that's only on the margins. More often, it makes sense to bring in new coaches with new players. Though for what it's worth, very, very few of them have the résumé that Perry Watson did in 1991.

So don't be saying that Coach Watson got a job because of me. You've got it backwards: I'm here right now, writing this book, having this career, having this life, because of Perry Watson. And I'm just one of many—players, coaches, scouts, broadcasters—who can say that.

Perry Watson isn't just a great basketball coach. Perry Watson is a hero.

Now let's get back to the real villain. The NCAA.

WE WERE aware of everything at Michigan. Sophomore year, we started wearing plain blue shirts during our warm-ups, shirts that didn't say "Nike" or "Michigan." We had become a valuable brand, but we had no way to take advantage of that. The shirts were our silent protest.

Other than that, there weren't many ways to get around the sense of injustice that we—and so many other college players before, during, and after our time—felt stepping onto courts in front of thousands of screaming fans, in front of millions of people watching on television. Regardless of everything, our pockets weren't getting filled with money, and it seemed like everyone else's were.

Still, I will say that I always found ways to keep a little bit of cash in my pocket and not feel so strapped. Every summer, and sometimes during school, I had one job or another. I had a paper route, I shoveled snow, I cut grass, I pumped gas. One summer I worked for Dave Bing at Bing Steel. I worked on the steel press and drove a forklift. It was one of the few places where no one cared that I was a basketball star. If I messed up the press, believe me, they didn't care who I was.

To supplement that, I'd find ways to hustle. If I needed a few chairs for my dorm room, so we could have somewhere to sit while we played video games, I'd "borrow" them from Chrisler Arena. Sometimes, like countless other people in the hood, I'd play the numbers, making a little extra here and there. One time in the summer after my sophomore year, I got invited to a dice game, got lucky, and won enough for a down payment on a new Honda Accord. I woke my mom up when I got home at 4:00 a.m. to tell her she had to take me to the dealership first thing.

I was also like any kid. If my mom had a little extra, she would throw me twenty bucks. Or my uncles did, or Uncle Ed. They helped to make sure that I could at least put gas in the Accord. Or even if I couldn't afford diamond earrings, I could at least get the best cubic zirconia money could buy.

In college I also had the benefit of a Pell Grant, a federal grant that provides living expenses in college if you qualify financially. In my day, it was $2,500 a semester. I felt rich when my grant money arrived, and not because I'd use it on stupid things. I'd pay my rent, my beeper bill, my light bill. It was probably the biggest thing that kept me from getting desperate for cash at school. But not everyone knows about the Pell Grant, or successfully navigates the channels to receive it.

You hear those stories about players who get busted stealing laptops or jewelry or whatever? They're not doing that because they want to wear the jewelry, or play with new computers. They're doing it to sell the stolen items and get money. They're doing it because they're desperate for cash even though they are smack in the middle of that multibillion-dollar business called college basketball.

Those are the extreme cases, of course, but it all comes back to a simple fact: There are hundreds of less fortunate kids who play big-time college sports. They help bring in millions and millions of dollars for their schools and the NCAA, and they don't see a dime of it. They come to schools with the expectation that they will spend the bulk of their time, and their focus, on their sport, both because that's the commitment they make when they accept a scholarship and because it's their dream to play in college and maybe the pros. (The reality is that only a tiny percentage of them will actually make it to the pros. The rest will be left behind. Maybe with a degree, maybe not.)

I'm talking about big-time college sports here: Division I football and basketball. Nothing against young athletes who play other sports, but with a few exceptions they don't bring in money the way football and basketball do. In fact, the revenue-generating sports pay for the non-revenue-generating sports. So with much respect

"1982"

As a nine-year-old, I passed a lot of notes in class, such as "Do you like me?" with three boxes to check: "Yes," "No," or "Maybe." I also rocked the turtleneck for school pictures.

Cleaner than the Board of Health (prom 1991).

My family: A circle of strength, founded on faith, joined in love, and kept by God. BACK ROW: Kev, me, and Bill. FRONT ROW: Ma, Grammie, and Tammy.

At the Southwestern alumni game, with my brother Howard Eisley; my godfather, Dave Bing; and father figure Perry Watson.

My brothers from another mother. We shocked the world!

Coach Fish, always the teacher, helping me become a student of the game.

Cutting down the net in 1992 before heading to the Final Four.

Naughty by Nature picnic '93, 118th Street, New Jersey.

Illmatic with Nas in '94.

BELOW: With my childhood idol, Magic Johnson, at Detroit Southwestern.

SOUTHWESTERN HIGH SCHOOL
APRIL 1993

Draft day . . . where dreams come true.

ABOVE RIGHT:
I was so very fortunate for my
childhood idol Isiah to become my
mentor. An original Bad Boy, and
now a very appreciated
JRLA supporter.

In Indiana, when Larry Bird
was my coach from 1997
to 2000, he had my back
when no one else did. A true
legend—as a player, a coach,
and a man.

So blessed to be one of the 4,000 individuals to have played in an NBA game.

I've been covering the NBA Finals for television since 2002. Here I am on the ABC/ESPN set with the Worldwide Leader.

DETROIT

Jimmy Walker with the Pistons. We're the only father/son duo to score 10,000-plus points in the NBA.

With my brother, friend, and mentor: "The Sports Guy" Bill Simmons.

Celebrating life with my Queen Krissy.

So fortunate to have amazing kids who are intelligent, athletic, and stylish (Gracie, LaDarius, and Mariah).

Just being silly with my beautiful daughters.

Uncle Len swung an iron fist for discipline that he called "hani goshi."

With President Barack Obama,
who is also a fellow lefty.

The talented Uncle Paramore representing
at the JRLA ribbon-cutting ceremony.
Have mind, will create!

JRLA inaugural class of scholars ready to "Enter a Learner: Exit a Leader."

to the lacrosse players and the wrestlers and the volleyball players, they're not being taken advantage of in the same way. In life, everyone isn't treated equally in their jobs either. Get over it.

Football and basketball are the only college sports (along with to a lesser extent baseball and hockey, and obviously the best of the best in other sports) where athletes realistically can envision a professional career, or maybe an Olympic career or the like. Which brings me to a question: If you were in that situation, and you got up early one morning with nothing to do, would you be more likely to hit the library for three hours or go to the gym? You'd go to the gym, because that's what you're in school to do: to become the best athlete you can be and put yourself in position to make it to the next level. That's what your coaches ask you to do, what the administration expects you to do, and what the fans want you to do.

Okay, so if that makes sense, how can people crow about poor graduation rates and academic standards for college athletes? You can't make *two* things your *one* top commitment. If you're dedicated to your sport, academics are going to take a backseat. Particularly if you come from a high school that isn't the best of the best, it's all but impossible to keep up.

So we've got two problems. First, the athletes aren't getting paid, when everyone else is making money. And, second, the athletes are being expected to approach their sport like professionals, and to be conscientious and committed students. To me, those hypocrisies are at the core of what's fundamentally wrong with college sports.

There are two pretty simple solutions.

First, pay the athletes. Not a ridiculous sum of money, but a decent, modest payment that will give them some cushion in their bank account and let them share in the profits of the college sports machine. The money should come out of the budget for apparel and shoes, so it's self-sustaining within the athletic departments. Let's say $5,000 per semester, $10,000 a year for the top schools, and maybe somewhat less for smaller schools (who have less lucrative sponsorship deals). Maybe increase it a thousand per year so juniors and seniors make more than freshmen. That might even entice players who aren't the biggest pro prospects to stay in school and get closer to graduation. Is $10,000 a year enough to retire on? No. But it echoes the way things work in another system, baseball, where the minor leagues, not college ball, are the central feeders to the majors. Minor leaguers don't make much money. But they are paid, with the enticement that the better they are, the closer they'll get to real money in the big show. (Furthermore, in baseball, the union will pay for players to finish college. So when it doesn't work out for young pitchers or hitters on the diamond, they have something to fall back on afterward. Baseball: best union in sports.) For college athletes, payment would serve as an extra piece of their scholarship. Call it an athletic grant if that makes you feel better. And don't stop the Pell Grant Program. Let the programs supplement each other, to make sure the neediest players are getting everything they might need.

Next, let college athletes major in sports. Now, at a lot of schools, there are sports management degrees and kinesiology degrees and other programs like that. Take the curriculum a step further. Acknowledge that playing their sport is the athlete's focus, and then build a modified academic program around that. They would get credit for being on a team and have a schedule that touches on the rest of the sports world: training, coaching, nutrition, management, administration, and so on. All these areas are exploding with innovation. There's plenty to learn about and contribute to. Athletes wouldn't be forced to major in sports, but the program would be available for students who want it.

People might complain that it's unfair to offer athletes something special, but where in life don't people who are doing something special get something special? Nonathletes don't need to worry about athletes suddenly graduating and taking their jobs. Believe me, if a basketball player is hired for a job after college and he doesn't cut it, he'll get fired just like anyone else. But, by participating in a program that helps him stay in school and get a degree in the first place, athletes increase their potential to be better at future jobs.

If big-time college sports made those two changes—pay players and let them major in sports—it wouldn't be a perfect situation. But it would be better.

THE NCAA is never going to be able to erase our history. But they have changed it. Because of allegations involving one individual, not an entire team, there's no evidence of our legacy at Michigan. Other schools that have had similar issues after Final Four runs— Memphis and UMass come to mind—still have their banners up. Ours was taken down.

And then there's everything else that came after. The investigation into Ed Martin lasted years, spoiling the life of a man who'd done a tremendous amount of good in Detroit. Ed was going to co-operate with the government in the beginning, and then he wasn't. The case took a lot of twists and turns. Then came the biggest twist of all: Chris lied to the grand jury. It was a move that revealed Chris's lack of street smarts. Everyone else told the truth. All he had to do was the same thing. Instead, he lied, saying that he didn't know who Ed Martin was (when there were a hundred pictures of them together). To make it even worse, he held a press conference where he accused Ed of helping kids when they were young so he could cash in on that love and support later in their careers.

That press conference had devastating effects. First, it was the final blow to a relationship that had begun to collapse after Chris declared for the NBA Draft and Ed gave him that big loan. How do I know the details of the money Ed gave Chris? Because Ed told me so, in the summer of 1993, in the kitchen of my mom's house. He came over to see if I could help him find Chris, who had changed his phone number after signing a $75 million contract and wasn't getting back to Ed about paying him back. Suddenly, years later, he was watching that press conference, watching a kid he'd looked after for almost twenty years disavow him, and looking at jail time to boot. Think about that relationship, going back to our teenage years. Besides the food and clothes and support throughout the years, Ed paid for the party at the 1940 Chop House when Chris announced he was going to Michigan. Even before that, Chris and I were at Ed's house when we decided we were going to go to Michigan together. The list goes on and on and on, all the way to the big money that Ed loaned Chris that ultimately got him in trouble— money that Chris may have eventually paid only 10 percent back on, tops, even as he went on to almost $200 million in his career. Ed died in 2003—while he was awaiting sentencing. They said it was a pulmonary embolism. I'm no cardiologist, but that sounds a lot like a broken heart.

Chris's statement also hurt and disappointed me. I knew the truth about their relationship. And I'd spoken to Chris about what had happened, and Chris had always told me he'd take care of it. Ultimately, though, it involved a lot of money, and you know what Biggie said about that. But at its heart, Ed's deal with us kids was simple, and unspoken. Let me help you, he said, to make things a little better for you. As far as payback was concerned, if someday we had some bigger bills in our pocket, we weren't expected to go to Mr. Ed's house and give him a brown paper bag. We were supposed to spot the next kid who needed a coat, the next kid who needed some sneakers, the next time we could bring a few seafood pizzas to a practice, and do it ourselves. White people call that paying it forward. On the block, we call it looking out—and keeping it real.

Watching Chris at that press conference, almost ten years after our last game at Michigan, was a reminder of how much had changed since the last night of the Fab Five in that hotel room in New Orleans. A night, ironically enough, that Chris probably still wishes could be erased from history. That night the focus changed for Chris and for me. We were going to play professional basketball in the NBA. We were going to make a lot of money.

Exactly as I'd planned it that day in the dusty film room at St. Cecilia's.

THIRD QUARTER

The NBA

Life

8. What the NBA Can Teach You About Life, Luck, and Fate

I made the first mistake of my pro basketball career before it began.

I started it a year too late.

In 1993, when Chris Webber decided to go pro, he was the first college sophomore to be taken first overall in the NBA Draft since Magic Johnson. He was at the start of a new wave. Allen Iverson and Elton Brand—two more sophomores to go first overall—would follow him over the next few years. Also during that time, Kevin Garnett and Kobe went to the draft directly from high school. Today, even with the minimum-age limit on the draft, it's almost guaranteed that a freshman or a foreign player will be picked first. It's the new standard, and it started with a member of the Fab Five.

But I didn't see that trend coming in 1993. I also didn't see what my best move was. Even though we were losing our best player, and even though my sophomore year had shown me how messed up the system was around us and how it could spoil the fun we were having, I was still a rah-rah college guy. I believed in the meaning of the Fab Five, in what I felt we represented. Call me an idealist. Juwan was, too. We both could have left alongside Chris, and could have been drafted in the top ten. Instead, we went back to school.

We had the fairy-tale ending written in our minds. We would be the underdogs again, without Chris, and bring home the title for Coach Fisher. The one I'd promised him as soon as the Carolina game had ended.

Well, fairy tales are great, but they don't come with a check at the end of the rainbow. We eventually got paid, and paid a lot, but at that time we were two guys still driving old beat-up cars and scraping together pizza money. Furthermore, we ran the risk of getting injured or something happening that would change our NBA chances. Frankly, we made a dangerous decision.

We actually had a great season our junior year. We were ranked all season, as high as third, and second in the Big Ten, and we made another good run through the tournament. We came up one game short of a third Final Four, losing to the eventual national champions for the third straight year. This time it was Nolan Richardson's Arkansas Razorbacks, cheered on by a crowd that included none other than the president of the United States, Bill Clinton.

Despite all that success, the season was definitely less magical than the others. We were over being campus celebrities. We lived way off campus, and hung out at Eastern more than ever. (Our spot over there was the Spaghetti Bender.) Juwan and I were ready for the pro life, and we started prepping for the draft right after the season. The problem was, my third season hadn't done me any favors as far as setting me up as an NBA prospect. With Chris gone, I had moved from point guard to playing on the wing, with Dugan Fife, who was a year behind us, running the offense. My scoring and rebounding numbers went up, but I also lost my unique role as a six-foot-eight point guard in the fashion of Magic Johnson and Steve Smith (as well as Penny Hardaway, who'd been drafted two spots after C-Webb, and then traded for him). My profile for scouts in the NBA became muddled. You'd think versatility would be good, but in my case, I think it actually made me a less distinctive prospect.

While Juwan would probably tell you he should have left earlier, too, junior year only raised his profile. In particular, he was a total monster in the tournament, winning the most outstanding player in the region even though we didn't win our bracket. He showed he could step right into Chris's shoes and handle the load up front basically on his own. Juwan got drafted fifth, by Washington.

I think a year earlier I would have gone in the top seven. In 1994, I slipped to thirteen, the end of the lottery, becoming the newest member of the Denver Nuggets.

I still managed to make a splash at the draft. If you were watching that night in June 1994, I'm guessing you remember my red double-breasted, pique-lapel, custom-made pin-striped suit. It's still in all the Top 10 lists of the most legendary—okay, maybe infamous—NBA Draft ensembles in history. I'm still proud of it. And I can answer a question you've had on your minds for a few decades now. "Why, Jalen? Why?" Because I thought I was going to be drafted seventh, by the Los Angeles Clippers, whose primary team color is red. I'd had a good workout for them, and they'd told me that there was a good chance they were going to pick me. Admit it—that suit would have looked even more fly with a red Clippers hat to top it off. Instead, I had to wear a white Nuggets hat with a navy-blue brim. It was not a total disaster but was not the perfect match I was going for. Either way, the suit distracted from the zit I had under my eye that night. And though Lamond Murray, the Clippers' first pick, had a pretty good NBA career, there are no pictures of him on draft night living on as part of Internet lore.

Grant Hill went third that year, to my hometown Pistons. Now a guy who I had long seen as a rival from the other side of the tracks was headed to my turf to start on his NBA path.

I was headed to the Rocky Mountains, at long last fulfilling my destiny. Though for the record, the kid who thought he knew everything (me) knew nothing about what was in store.

I'VE BEEN in my fair share of fights in my lifetime. When I was a kid, practically one a week on almost every corner of west Detroit. By high school, and then college, the pace slowed to once in a while. I don't know what would have happened to me if I grew up today, rather than a few decades ago, because now it seems like every brother on the street has a gun or access to a gun, and fights escalate a whole lot differently. It was also before social media, so nobody was taking pictures or videos of fights on phones, and tweeting them out or posting them. Back then, you'd rush someone, or get rushed, and then life would continue. Fights were a natural outgrowth of the trash-talk and the language of the hood. A lot of us were frustrated about a lot of things. Sometimes it got heated. And then it was over.

At Michigan, the handful of skirmishes and brawls I got in stayed under the radar, in part because my role in them was usually quick. Was I tough? Sure, but I was also lucky. I was left-handed, and no one ever expects that your first punch is going to come from the other side. It's really pretty simple. You aim for one spot, right on the cheekbone. If you hit it with your middle finger, you're gonna pop blood, and that usually ends things right there. Even for tough brothers, the sight of their own blood usually slows the argument down enough for clearer heads to prevail and for people to break it up.

With that said, let me take you back to the summer of 1994, right after I got drafted. I'm back in Detroit, living large with my first six-figure paycheck in the works. Once a month, there was this party in town called "Soul Night" at the State Theatre. The guys and the girls would go to the beauty shop and the hair salon, get suited and booted, and head out to the theater. I remember I was driving a new car, a burgundy Suburban that I had tricked out with TVs in the back. This was before flat-screen monitors—I had actual TVs put in. I was Inspector Gadget. No idea was too much for my ride. I dubbed it "the Ice Box."

Anyway, a whole bunch of us went to Soul Night, and we ended up getting into an altercation with some other dudes. It was probably over some girls—I honestly don't remember the cause. What I do remember is that the Suburban turned out to be a hell of a getaway car. To get out of there before the cops came and my name surfaced, I actually jumped I-75 to take us south of town. And we made it. Phew, no problem, right? Wrong. As soon as I woke up that next morning, I knew something was not right with my shoulder. I called the new mentor in my life, my agent, Norm Nixon, the former Lakers and Clippers great. I'd picked Norm to be my agent for a few reasons: one, I wanted a black agent and, two, I already had my eye on the entertainment space, and Norm was an L.A. guy who was married to the famous actress and dancer Debbie Allen. (Who I will forever be indebted to for giving me my first facial. Hundreds more have followed.) Anyway, that day on the phone, Norm was as smooth as ever. He said, "Get out here, we'll get you looked at, no one will know anything."

This could never happen in today's world. News of an NBA draft pick getting in a fight would be on Twitter within seconds. I'm sure someone would grab a video and put that up as well. Then the mainstream media would get wind of it, and it would blow up.

But back in 1994, a week after the fight, I was quietly on a plane to L.A. I spent the rest of the summer quietly rehabbing this shoulder injury that no one, including the Nuggets, would ever find out about. Plus being out there was an opportunity to learn a bit about a town that had always intrigued me, with Magic Johnson and Showtime and everything surrounding that. I signed my six-year rookie contract shortly before training camp started, and reported to Denver 100 percent.

No harm, no foul. Right?

AS WILD as everything around the Fab Five became, the basketball experience at Michigan was actually pretty similar to mine at Southwestern. I was on a great team, filled with stars who all knew their roles, who won a lot of games. I'd played in three straight championship games in high school, followed by two straight in college.

Then I became a professional basketball player.

The best 450 players in the world distributed across 30 teams (when I started, it was 27), playing 82 games every season. In every one of those games, there's gonna be a winner, and there's gonna be a loser. Which means that for a lot of players, the NBA is the first place in their entire basketball careers that they lose games on a regular basis. In my rookie season in Denver, we won 41 games and we lost 41 games. Actually, we lost 44 if you include the three-game sweep in the opening round of the playoffs against David Robinson and the Spurs. Either way, that's more games than I had lost in my high school, college, and AAU careers combined.

On the one hand, I was one of the lucky rookies. Our team was competitive, I played in almost every game, and I started almost half of them at point guard. I still own the Nuggets rookie assist record.

That said, taking the long view of things, it wasn't so great. We had three coaches in one season. Dan Issel started, then he got burned out, had some issues, and quit. Gene Littles coached us for about a month as an interim. Then Bernie Bickerstaff, who was also the general manager, took over on the bench and led us to a strong finish and the playoffs. Each of those guys had their own views of every player on the roster, and their own ideas about the best way to play. As a rookie, I was basically like a high school freshman, paying my dues and proving myself every day. How can anyone do that effectively with a new boss almost every month?

I've thought a lot about what might have happened if I had gone out a year earlier, and ended up on another team that wasn't so in flux. I don't know if it would have been any better; but I do know it taught me a lesson about the role of luck and fate in an NBA career. Get put in the right situation, with the right coaching and support around you, and it can do unspoken wonders for your career.

Remember this: Right now, far away from the cameras and the reporters, there are NBA players that you barely pay any attention to who are working on their games with the help of great coaches and organizations. Then there are other players languishing on teams in transition, teams with assistant coaches who spend their time worrying about what they're going to do at the end of the season when their boss is fired. As a young player, being part of a good system can change your career. These days, how many guys that you have never heard of have gone to the Spurs and become productive players for a great team? Almost too many to count.

Unfortunately, as a rookie back then, I was a few years away from the good things that come with being in a great system.

TO BE fair, my timing wasn't all bad. I got into the NBA the last year before they imposed a tighter rookie salary cap, meaning I got a huge deal right off the bat: six years, $10 million guaranteed. That was a hell of a lot of money, but remember (and too many NBA players—past, present, and future—forget this) that almost half of that goes to taxes, and another big chunk goes to your agent. It's really $5 million. Again, a ton of cash, but half of what it sounds like.

One of the first things I did was buy a house in Englewood, Colorado, a suburb of Denver. From the start, I wanted to put my money into things I could understand. Not just stocks and bonds and mumbo jumbo that I didn't know anything about. A house. Everyone wants to buy their mom a house, too. Mine didn't want one. She wanted to stay in Detroit. Eventually I was able to convince her to let me get her a condo in the suburbs and, years later, the suburban house she lives in today. That took care of Mom.

Then there were the other people I was going to help out. All twenty of them. Well, at least twenty. It's not a stretch to say that at some point, everyone I knew from Detroit got at least a little love out of that contract.

Why so many? Because in my view, they all deserved it as

much as me. A village of people—uncles, aunts, neighbors, teachers, mentors, friends—had been a part of making sure I didn't take the wrong path and that my talents weren't wasted. They'd each been a brick in my success. Now, I'd hit the lottery for everyone, not just for myself. So there was help with people's mortgages, their car leases, their loans, their tuitions. For younger folks, my philosophy was that I'd rather teach them how to fish than simply buy them fish. If you brought me into it, I had a stake in it. I wanted to know: What are we going to do to use this leg up, the money you get, to give you the next leg up?

That's the philosophy I used with my closest friends from Detroit, who came to Denver with me. Yes, I had a so-called entourage. For some reason, in sports, that term only gets used with black athletes. For white athletes, the term is just "staff." In both cases, it's friends and family who've come out to support you on this crazy journey that began the moment you were drafted. The moment you basically became your own multimillion-dollar company. And like any CEO, you need support.

The key with an entourage is to keep it close. Make sure it's populated only by people who've known you since the very beginning, not people who showed up when you had already started making waves as a pro prospect. That's the best way to guarantee trust, and to prevent your entourage from getting its own entourage, which is no good. You also don't want it to be too big. Keep it manageable. Most important, make sure that everyone actually has something to do.

For me it was about helping my friends make something of their own lives. For example, Rizz, who was into cooking, was my chef. And while I was playing ball, he was attending culinary school, with the goal that someday he could have his own catering business. Today, he does. Rizz grew up six or seven houses down the street from Uncle Paramore, and I've known him since we were kids. Then there was K-Nine, who had gone to Southwestern with me. His thing was staying in shape, so he was the trainer, working out alongside me, pushing me. My other boy Montez, or 'Tez, also went to Southwestern, and was my assistant. He was the guy making sure the gardener got let in and out, the contractor got what he needed, and was the person I could trust with business stuff when I wasn't around. He also hooked up the social end of things, making sure in this new city I wasn't going to be the guy standing in the middle of the club not knowing anybody. That stuff counted, too.

On the periphery were the businesspeople I was spending money with, the agents and the brokers and the deal makers, but they were an outer layer. In my house in Englewood, it was me and my three boys. We had made it big, together. A lot of the money went to the three *C*'s—clothes, clubs, and cars. Some of it was spent a little recklessly (okay, completely recklessly), like on the bracelet I called "the Mansion," because it was so expensive, and a few years later, when cell phones came out, on a Vertu phone. Those were probably the dumbest things I ever bought. Wearing the bracelet was basically an invitation for someone to rob me, and have you ever seen a Vertu phone? Still, I can't look back and say I regret buying those items. I was just me letting the world know—and proving to myself—that I wasn't poor anymore. If I wanted something that only rich people could have, I was rich now and I could have it. People who aren't from the hood might roll their eyes at the huge diamond earrings that were in my ears, but for me, they represented something priceless.

One expenditure from those early days I'll *definitely* never regret is getting veneers. Look at that photo of me at the draft, with the red suit. It's the last time anyone would ever be able to call me "rock teeth," because a few weeks later, I got them fixed.

Smile for the camera. The NBA was calling.

ON THE one hand, it's one of the most elite clubs in the world. Four hundred and fifty guys, almost all of them making over $1 million a year to play basketball for a living. Private planes, catered meals, anything and everything you need to be the best athlete you can be.

On the other hand, the NBA is just like any other club, or community, or job. With traditions, hierarchies, pecking orders, and certain ways of doing things that, as a player, you have to figure out for yourself. In the gym and the locker room, there are no agents or entourages to protect you, and they wouldn't impress anybody anyway. There's only the dozen-plus guys on the team. They are the only ones who get to wear the uniform, who get the seats on the bench, whose names get called to go into the games.

The group I was a part of was an interesting mix. There were a few other lottery picks just ahead of me. LaPhonso Ellis, who had been the star at Notre Dame when I was a freshman, was hurt all year my rookie season. Rodney Rogers had been drafted by the team the year before me. Both of those guys looked out for me. And they were also happy to see me take over the rookie duties. like carrying the bags off the plane, bringing doughnuts to morning practice, and so forth. Then there were the less glamorous duties, like getting ready to chill in my hotel room, having my phone ring, and hearing the unmistakable African accent on the other end of the line.

"HEY ROOKIE! GOT TO MAKE A RUN FOR ME!"

Yes, Dikembe Mutombo may be more than seven feet tall, he may have built hospitals in the Congo, but that doesn't mean he doesn't need protection like any other brother trying to stay warm on some cold nights on the road. So I'd be the one who had to go outside and find a CVS pharmacy, buy a box of Magnums, and bring them up to his room.

Rookie life.

The most interesting guy on that Nuggets team was Mahmoud Abdul-Rauf, the point guard who a few years before had converted to Islam and changed his name from Chris Jackson. I liked being around him because I learned so much, not so much from what he had to say, but from what he had to do. He had Tourette syndrome and OCD (obsessive-compulsive disorder) issues, and for him to function and feel comfortable, everything around him had to be immaculate. He'd lay his shoes and socks down just so, his clothes down just so. Nothing could be folded or wrinkled at all. It was a fascinating thing to watch this guy deal with this disorder up close.

When I was there, he caused a big controversy by refusing to stand for the national anthem because doing so was at odds with his religious beliefs. We had a lot of conversations about it. I felt like a lot of what he and I were discussing in our hotel room or on team flights was more informed than any of the junk flying around about the situation in the press. The press didn't even notice he was doing it for weeks, let alone make a big deal out of it, until we played the Bulls, the best team in the league. I'd always been skeptical of the press, and their cluelessness didn't impress me in this case at all.

As teammates, we could exchange ideas and not get caught up in the outside controversy. To me, while I respect what he did and what he believed, the whole scenario didn't quite add up. At the time he was driving a yellow Lamborghini with no qualms. If he was enjoying the spoils of the NBA life in a free society, how does the national anthem offend him all of a sudden, while everything else about the life is okay? Eventually there was a compromise: Abdul-Rauf bowing his head and staying silent during the anthem.

The whole thing overshadowed what a great player he was— his handle, his ability to stop on a dime, pump fake, and then turn around and drain it was up there with anyone in the league. Along with Mutombo, he was probably the best player we had on the Nuggets those years, and one of the only veterans that I was able to connect with. Robert Pack, Bryant Stith, and Reggie Williams were all guards who I was competing for playing time with, and even though they had love for me, they couldn't really take me under their wing. I can't blame them for that; it was an early lesson in life in the NBA. I may have walked into the Nuggets' locker room feeling that I'd finally reached the pinnacle. But taking the next step, becoming a veteran, the most respected position of all in the league, was no guarantee.

In fact, in the NBA, nothing is guaranteed except the payday. Piss off the wrong teammate, the wrong assistant coach, or the wrong executive, and you can find yourself at the end of the bench, or worse. Just like in any job, the "politricks" can sometimes seem like everything.

There are no limits on the tricks and moves that people can play. And no limits to how fast your reality can change. In Denver, I learned that quickly—when Bernie Bickerstaff blew up the

Nuggets roster after my second season, 1995–96. The team wouldn't make the playoffs again until Carmelo Anthony showed up in 2003. Meanwhile, as part of the breakup of the team, I was traded to Indiana.

And that's when I really got tested.

"CHRIS WEBBER and Juwan Howard are up here," the guy sitting across the desk from me said, raising his hand above his head. "And Jimmy King and Ray Jackson are down over here, out of the league."

He paused, coldly staring at me.

"Now *I'm* going to be the one to determine which way you go."

Ladies and gentlemen, one of basketball's most legendary coaches, Larry Brown.

He wasn't finished.

"If I want you to go up here," Larry raised his hand again, "you're going to have a long and successful career. If I decide you're going to go the other way, you might be out of the league before long."

I had come to Indiana feeling optimistic. I was back in the Midwest, closer to home, and coming to a team that had made the playoffs for seven straight seasons. Donnie Walsh, the highly respected personnel man for the Pacers, clearly saw something in me, making me the centerpiece of a package that he got in exchange for his starting point guard, Mark Jackson. What I didn't realize at the time of that last detail was the cross I had to bear in Indy. Mark Jackson was Larry Brown's favorite player, like a son to him, not to mention Reggie Miller's closest friend. And he was replaced, by me. What?

You thought in the pros, this kind of stuff wasn't supposed to matter? Welcome to Politricks 101.

Donnie Walsh had made a basketball decision to trade for me. The other key guys in the equation didn't like that, and they turned my first year in Indiana into a total mess before I could even figure out what was going on. Before the season started, we had an overseas trip with Seattle, and in one of the games I had something like twenty points and thirteen assists, completely lighting up the future Hall of Fame stud Gary Payton. It was preseason, but it was still basketball, and I figured I was on my way to big things. Wrong. In that first conversation we had, Larry Brown had let me know that *he* was in control with his comments about me, Chris, and Juwan, and he'd added that he was never a fan of the Fab Five, and didn't like what players like me represented in the league. Well, to this day, I'm not sure what he was talking about, because Mark Jackson was known for doing this shimmy after a big bucket or big play, and Reggie Miller was one of the biggest trash-talkers in the league. None of that mattered, though, because the head coach—the head "politrickian"—was the man in charge.

The first few games of the year, I was a reserve and played twenty to twenty-five minutes. Then we had a game against Washington, which meant we were playing against Chris and Juwan. I was excited to see those guys. We were talking on the phone before the game, talking trash about facing off against each other; it felt like it was going to be fun. Then Larry had to answer questions about the Fab Five before the game. He hated that. He got his revenge by playing me for all of four minutes. That became a pattern all year long. He'd play me for a stretch of games, and then I'd get a DNP ("did not play") or just garbage-time minutes. He was trying to destroy my confidence. He didn't know, first, that he wouldn't be able to do that, and, second, that he wouldn't change me one bit.

Meanwhile, the players on the team didn't do much to back me up, at least as far as I could tell. Reggie was the team's best player, a future Hall of Famer and the team captain. He was a leader who might have had some influence with the coach. But he wasn't my agent, and it wasn't his job to tell the coach who to play. Eventually, Reggie became a big-brother figure to me, but that year I was frustrated with the whole situation. The players knew inferior players were getting more time than me on the court, and nobody said a word.

My solution was simple: treat practice like games and work my ass off. Summoning anger for use on the basketball court had always been one of my biggest weapons. I'd be as loud and as brash and as dominating in practice as I could be. All the better if I was matched up against Reggie. It wasn't going to get any worse, and as long as my confidence stayed intact, I knew I'd be all right in the end. Even if Larry benched me every time we played in Detroit, in front of my friends and family, and even if he continued to try to mess with my head in every way he could. And there was something I knew was just as important. I never reacted in public, never lashed out or brought more controversy upon myself. That would have helped Larry Brown achieve what he wanted.

I could also take solace in the fact that the team, which had made it to the conference finals just two years earlier, was imploding on the court. Toward the end of the year, in the midst of one of my DNP stretches, I got called into Donnie Walsh's office. Maybe my stay in Indy was going to be short, I thought. Instead, Donnie said something I wasn't expecting: While Larry wasn't going to be around after the season, I was. He told me to keep practicing hard, because I was still in his plans.

My goal when I walked out of Donnie Walsh's office, late in that 1996–97 season, was to not become what Larry Brown wanted to make me. I didn't want to be a journeyman, a guy who flames out of the league in a few years. In my house in Indiana, I still had an unopened letter in a drawer from a guy who had been a two-time All-Star in the league. I hadn't gotten to that level yet.

I wouldn't have predicted that the guy to take me would be one of the greatest legends the game of basketball has ever known.

And a white one at that.

9. The Three Things That Mean More than Anything in the NBA

You can never get away from politricks in the NBA. If a team ever did, I can guess where they'd be: definitely still playing in May and June, and probably standing on a podium getting the Larry O'Brien Trophy at the end of the season.

It's not easy to get to that place. I guarantee you that every great team that's won a championship over the last several decades—or, in a lot of cases, come damn close—had some common ingredients. You always want to keep these things in mind, no matter what opinion about a player, a team, a game, or a series some guy gabbing on TV is promoting (including me).

Fate.

Coaching.

Talent.

These concepts are often misunderstood. Let's try to get a handle on them.

SPEAKING OF fate, let me go back to my college days for a second. I loved playing against the biggest names, like Coach K and Bob

Knight, because I always felt like I was part of the long tradition of basketball when they were involved—living legends who'd been trained by the legends who came before them. When we played Duke or Indiana, I felt like I was supposed to be playing them, and beating them. I'd go up to them, shake their hand, pay tribute, and then go about my business of trying to win. I did the same thing when I spotted someone in the stands, an alumnus or a parent of a player or a legend who was in town and wanted to catch the local Big Ten matchup.

Sophomore year, we lost to Duke early, but then rolled off nine wins in a row heading into our Big Ten opener at Purdue. Purdue came in undefeated. It was Glenn Robinson's first year on the team, and he was already playing like a stud. The Big Dog (a future Michigan dad—Hail!) had thirty points that night, but we won the game. Afterwards, while everyone was celebrating and heading off the court, I went over to the corner of the stands, where I'd spotted an even bigger star sitting and watching the game—none other than the immortal Larry Bird.

I'd actually *almost* met Larry Bird a few years earlier when, as a reward for winning one of our city titles, Coach Watson had taken our team to a Pistons–Celtics game and got us into the locker rooms after the game. Mike Ham and I saw that trip as an opportunity to prove that we really were—as we told everyone in school—six feet nine inches tall. Well, everyone knew Larry Legend was six nine, so we slyly wandered up next to his locker, and measured ourselves. Forget it—we weren't even close. Eventually, I got myself listed at six eight, and we will leave it at that.

But back to the Purdue game. It was Bird's first year of retirement, and he was living in his hometown of French Lick, scouting for the Celtics. Purdue was in his neighborhood. I went over to him, shook his hand, told him how much I appreciated his coming to the game. I had been a Magic Johnson fan growing up, and part of following the Magic–Bird rivalry was understanding how amazing Bird was. Bird was the kind of enemy I admired and respected, like Christian Laettner. Larry Bird may have broken my heart many times (including with that steal against the Pistons in the '87 conference finals), but not before establishing himself in my mind as the greatest small forward ever to play the game.

When I shook his hand that night in 1993, I obviously had no idea that four years later, the Legend would make his full-time return to the game as the coach of the Pacers. And that, apparently, he'd tell Donnie Walsh the same thing that he'd told the Celtics' front office after that game at Purdue.

He—*Larry Bird*—wanted me on his team.

THE MOST overlooked factor that goes into life in the NBA is fate. I say fate rather than luck, because it's not right to say that players like LeBron James, Kobe Bryant, Michael Jordan, Magic Johnson, and Larry Bird are lucky, but fate still played a role in their careers. I define fate as the part of the game that the competitor has no control over: the draft lottery, injuries, a freak play. They all can matter as much as skill.

For example, before free agency, an athlete's career could be defined by who drafted him. If you got drafted by a team from a small city, you were going to be a small-market player for as long as that team wanted you. In the age of free agency, players who last in the league have more freedom to choose their teams, but they still don't have control over everything. Injuries can turn franchise players into mere mortals—it's amazing how much can go up in the smoke of a blown-out knee. It's a reminder that a huge piece of success in sports is simply fate.

That reality applies to championship teams as much as anything else. Teams have to stay healthy. They have to have a thousand little things go their way over the course of the season and the postseason. The big shots have to go in, the big plays have to go their way. Though if you look back you'll find that, more often than not, fate smiled down on the teams who deserved it. Like Ray Allen's famous prayer at the end of Game 6 of the 2013 Finals. Was it a lucky shot? Or was it one of the best shooters in NBA history having the ball in his hands and getting the perfect opportunity, after one of the best players in the league, Chris Bosh, found a way to get it to him? Yes, it was fate that the ball went in to extend that game, and the series. But Allen, Bosh, and the Heat had done everything they could to get it to that point, and to put themselves in position for fate to smile upon them.

You can argue about the importance of fate the next time you run out of topics with a friend at a sports bar. (Talk loudly—tell people you got the argument from my book!) I'll say this: The first three seasons of my career, largely for reasons that were out of my control, were nowhere near as successful as I expected them to be. Then came the stroke of good fate: Larry Bird gets hired to coach the Pacers, giving me a new lease on my NBA life.

By that point, I'd learned enough about pro basketball to know that when fate smiles down upon you, you do everything you can to capitalize.

. . .

THE SUMMER league is for rookies and undrafted free agents. Not many guys who've been in the league for a few years play in the games. But in the summer of 1997, I saw the summer league as a huge opportunity to showcase my game for Larry Legend and his new staff, and even more important, let them know that I was ready to do anything I had to do to take my career to the next level.

Larry had reached out to me immediately when he'd taken the job, letting me know that he had a sense of what had happened the year before with the previous coach, that he had always liked my game since watching me in college and wanted to work with me to make me a great pro. It was a quick phone call, no longer than a minute, but it sent a message to me. From then on, my outlook on playing with the Pacers did a complete 180. Sometimes it's the simple things—in this instance, just one phone call.

At the summer league, I got acquainted with Larry's top assistant and former teammate, a guy by the name of Rick Carlisle. Now, if you think that the Hick from French Lick and the Rose from west Detroit were a strange combination, you'd probably think Carlisle— who looks like a cross between a farm boy and a drill sergeant— and I were an even less likely pair. But there's no doubt that I owe more to both of them than anyone else for the success I had in the NBA. From the summer league to the time training camp started in that '97–'98 season and beyond, Carlisle had me doing drills, watching game film, and working overtime in practice to develop my game further. He helped me strengthen my post game in particular, where I could exploit my size advantage over a lot of guards, making me a better player overall.

Larry Bird, meanwhile, was the overseer, the CEO of the team.

In some crazy way, we were a natural pair. First off, he was one of the great trash-talkers in NBA history. Talk to anyone who went up against him in his era, and they'll tell you how much he dominated the mental part of the game as fiercely as he took care of business with his jumper and unparalleled all-around arsenal. I bonded with him as much as I had with any other coach in my life. I appreciated that he told me he was a big fan of my dad as a player, and he's one of the smartest guys I've met in basketball. In meetings in his office or conversations on the road, we talked about a million things, on a basketball level and a personal level.

The result was that Bird and Carlisle had not just my respect, but my trust. I would do anything for them, as I had for Perry Watson and Steve Fisher. They didn't immediately turn me into the team's featured star or anything like that. Larry said he was going to coach for three seasons, and no more. The first two seasons, I started one game, total. Every other game, I was the team's sixth man, averaging twenty-five minutes a game or less, averaging ten shots a game or less.

What they did do was turn around the team. With almost the same roster—plus the reacquisition, ironically, of Mark Jackson—they guided the team that missed the playoffs in 1997 to the seventh game in the conference finals in 1998 against Michael Jordan and the Bulls. The next year, in the strike-shortened season, we lost in the same round to the Knicks. Then, finally, everything came together in the third year.

It was a huge lesson for me: how much coaching can make a difference in a career. The impact of a figure like Larry Bird was totally undeniable.

He coached us two wins short of an NBA title.

. . .

THIS NEVER fails to trick even the biggest basketball fans. Over the last thirty-four NBA seasons, three men have combined to win more than two-thirds of the titles, twenty-three in all. Those three men also have collectively made the Finals another seven times. All told, twenty-eight out of thirty-three seasons, one of them was either raising the trophy, or right there, missing by just a game or two. Who are they? No, not Magic, not Michael, not Larry, not Kobe, not Tim Duncan, not LeBron. They've all won multiple titles, but even the best players can't dominate three-plus decades that dramatically.

The three guys aren't players. They're the three best coaches—check that, the three best leaders—of the modern age of basketball: Phil Jackson, Gregg Popovich, and Pat Riley.

Now let's roll back the timeline even further. This one's easier. One guy was at the helm of the team that won almost half of the NBA titles from the mid-'50s to the early '80s: the legendary Red Auerbach, the coach, general manager, and president of the Celtics.

Everywhere else people look at successful companies or organizations and give credit, rightfully, to the leadership, to the CEO, the president, the chairman or chairwoman, whatever. In basketball, it should be the same. Over NBA history, great organizations like the Celtics, the Lakers, and the Spurs have remained a cut above everyone else because of one reason: their leadership.

Boston had Auerbach, who ran that organization forever, and brought in everyone from Bill Russell to John Havlicek to Larry Bird and Kevin McHale.

The Lakers had Dr. Jerry Buss, who as chairman, a position less involved in basketball than Red's, brought in a couple of different brilliant "basketball CEOs," if you will—Riley, and later Jackson—to nurture superstars like Magic and Kobe.

The Spurs have been one of the NBA's very best teams for almost two decades, with Popovich at the helm and some very smart people in the front office alongside him. Do you realize the Spurs have won at least fifty games (or, in shortened seasons, would have) in every one of Pop's nineteen seasons as coach? Yes, players like Tim Duncan are critical—the Spurs wouldn't have won five titles without him—but Duncan has stayed in San Antonio because he loves Pop. Now, don't forget the Spurs were fortunate to have the top pick the year Duncan was coming out. It was a season when David Robinson got hurt, and so San Antonio fell into the lottery. Pop never hesitates to remind people of that good fate. Regardless, fate doesn't explain the smart focus on international talent before the rest of the league, and also a progressive, forward-thinking mentality that led to the hiring of Becky Hammon as the NBA's first full-time female assistant coach.

*I'm a huge fan of the best players I've rooted for,
played against, and covered. But in basketball, great
leadership and guidance can make all the difference.
Michael Jordan and Shaquille O'Neal and Kobe Bryant
didn't win a title until Phil Jackson came along, and
LeBron won his titles when he went to Miami to play
for Pat Riley and his protégé, Erik Spoelstra. Even if
you have a Hall of Fame superstar on your team, the
coach needs to be the leader of a locker room. It's his
personality, his dynamic, his way of going about the
business of winning, that sets the tone.*

*So, what's more important—the superstar player or the
superstar coach? To me, the evidence points to the coach.*

LARRY BROWN wasn't the kind of leader I'm talking about when
I was with the Pacers. He couldn't have been if he was taking it
personally when Donnie Walsh made a legitimate basketball trade
to get me and spent his time trying to mess with my head. Players from the Pistons won't admit it because they won a title with
him, and players from the Pacers probably don't want to admit it,
but the locker room wasn't devoted to Larry Brown—it was united
against him. In the locker room, even his most "loyal" guys, including Reggie Miller, would be saying things like "Hey, we hate
this guy. Let's take our energy out on winning the game—not for
him, but for us." That was the underlying theme of that team, and
a basis of the success that it had.

Let me make one more point about Larry Brown: The guy coached eighteen straight seasons in the NBA for six different teams, not once taking a year off. First off, if you're a player with that kind of record, then you're not a Hall of Famer, you're a journeyman. Second, in coaching, you don't do that by luck. You plan it. Donnie Walsh knew Larry was done at the end of the 1996–97 season because Larry was already talking to the 76ers about coming to Philly. Larry got in trouble in Detroit because they found out he was talking to Cleveland during the NBA Finals. If a coach gets a new job right after the season ends, he's been working on it during the season. Those rumors find their way into the locker room even before they find their way into the media. Players know when their coach isn't totally devoted to them, when he isn't being straight with them. Peter Vecsey was right to call him "Next Town Brown." Keep getting those checks, Larry.

Coaches like Phil Jackson, Pat Riley, and Gregg Popovich aren't like that. They build organizations, win championships, and then work to maintain their excellence. They get great players to buy into their ideas.

I never played for those three guys, but playing for Larry Bird was its own lesson in tremendous leadership. He was the overseer who didn't say too much, who didn't jump into the fray all that often. If there were ten seconds left and we had the ball down by one, Larry might say something in the huddle, but it would be Carlisle, the offensive coordinator, drawing up the play. But because of how we knew he led the team in every other way—both emotionally all season long, and in plenty of other ways on the bench during games—there was never a doubt that he was in charge.

Bird also wasn't afraid to admit his mistakes. In the 1998 conference finals, we took the Bulls to seven games, one of two teams to do that in their championship years (the Knicks did it in '92 as well). We were up real big in the first half of Game 7. At one point, while we were humming, I hit two straight jumpers, they called timeout, and Larry took me out. We lost that big lead in three minutes, and I barely played the rest of the game. Afterwards, as I was getting on the bus for the airport, Larry came up to me and apologized. He said, "You know what, I'm sorry. I blew it. We tried to go defense. I should have left you in there. We needed another ball handler, and you were making shots. I love you. You're my guy."

Can't ask for more honesty from a coach than that.

A lot of Larry's "guys" have been like me, guys who were perceived as projects or rough around the edges, but with tremendous potential. Lance Stephenson is a recent example—he has a different personality from mine, a different game from mine, but Larry saw his potential, and he went from a fringe player to one of the Pacers' key pieces before he decided to leave for Charlotte. There are even more extreme examples from other coaches. Phil Jackson with Dennis Rodman. Pat Riley with all the crazy guys from junior colleges and the bargain bin he's had on the Knicks and the Heat. Pop with practically dozens of players he's brought to San Antonio. All players with tremendous talent who have thrived under strong leaders.

The same thing, by the way, applies to my favorite coaches in other sports, like Bill Parcells and Bill Belichick in football. Whether it was Lawrence Taylor or Randy Moss, those legends always found ways to get the best out of incredible talents who were different from everyone else.

I played for only one guy in the pros who was on that level. I would have run through a brick wall for Larry Bird. Still would. In the playoffs against the Knicks, he decided I was going for too many of my own buckets and not incorporating the team as much as I could on the second unit. In an interview with a newspaper, he called me "selfish." My response? I cut out the article and put it up on my locker. If the Legend thought I was selfish, I was going to make sure I didn't forget it.

That's one more thing that great coaches have. The aura. Bird earned it as a player. Some of the other greats built it on the sidelines. But it's critical for gaining the respect of all the players in the locker room and getting them to follow you to the promised land.

Getting all the way there is about the hardest thing to do in the NBA.

LARRY BIRD'S three short seasons as Pacers coach were each very different. The first year, he revived a team that Larry Brown had driven into the ground and brought us to within one game of the NBA Finals. The second year, he had to deal with the strangeness of the lockout-shortened fifty-game season and, again, got us to the conference finals. The third year, having decided that the current team wasn't ever going further than that, he changed things up.

Namely, he turned the car keys over to me.

The team had gotten a little bit stagnant, a little bit too predictable, a little bit old. Reggie Miller is one of the greatest shooters in the history of basketball, Rik Smits was a massive center who could dominate a game in spurts, but beyond those players there weren't enough options to provide variety on offense. So Larry, Rick Carlisle, and the staff came up with the idea to move me to the starting lineup to play small forward. Then, when the second unit came out, they'd keep me on the court as the point guard.

As the season started, everything felt fresh, including our court. It was the Pacers' first year in Conseco Fieldhouse after leaving Market Square Arena. We started out 7-7, but then got hot, particularly at home, at one point reeling off a twenty-five-game home-winning streak at our new house. Everyone we played knew we weren't the same old Pacers, and that was cool with me. On offense, Reggie didn't have the pressure of carrying the load by himself every night. During the season he and I were both averaging around thirty-seven minutes a game, with eighteen points per game each. As one of the youngest members of the team, my game matured as I played alongside veterans like Reggie, Mark Jackson, and the guy I called "Throwback," Chris Mullin. I improved my competitive edge—knowing how to play smart and win the head games—by combining what came naturally with tricks learned from these veterans.

Meanwhile, it was the first time in my NBA career that I was a focus of the offense. All that work I'd put in with Rick Carlisle, and the patience I'd shown, was paying dividends for me on one of the best teams in the league. True, there are a lot of guys in the league who can put up eighteen points a game, but to do it on a great team shows that you're a complete player. It also shuts up people like Larry Brown, who later claimed that he didn't put me in because I wouldn't play defense. If a team wins fifty-six games and gets the top seed in the conference, a guy playing thirty-seven minutes a game has to be playing some defense, don't you think? In the end, players and coaches around the league agreed. In 2000, I was named the NBA's Most Improved Player.

We got closer as a team, too. Travis Best was my best friend on the squad. I hung out a lot with the Davis "Brothers," Dale and Antonio. Mark Jackson, "Jax," was the kind of leader who got along with everyone and brought everyone closer together. Reggie and I got closer. I always appreciated that two years earlier, when I was coming off the bench, he had taken me on the plane with him to New York to the All-Star Game in appreciation for helping him, as an important teammate, play at a high level and get that honor. And in 2000, we clicked as a true two-man attack.

Despite all that, fans will remember that our playoff run that year almost ended before it started, when we played the Bucks the first round of the playoffs. The Bucks had a good thing going with George Karl coaching, and Glenn Robinson, Ray Allen, and Sam Cassell leading the way. They knew us well. They were in the same division and played us the year before in the playoffs. We swept them in '99, but in 2000, they stretched us to the full five games before my boy Travis Best drilled a three with sixteen seconds left in Game 5 to win it for us.

Larry Brown and the Sixers were next. We had also beaten them in the playoffs the year before, but I was still out for more vengeance. In Game 1, Reggie and I made NBA history, joining an elite group by each scoring forty points in the same playoff game. A few nights later, though, Matt Geiger and Reggie got into it, leaving Reggie suspended. The series went to six before we closed them out.

Next up were the conference finals and the Knicks, who the Pacers had battled in the playoffs since my college days. This was Patrick Ewing's last stand, and New York wasn't going to go down easy. I actually lost a tooth in one of the early games, and it was tooth-and-nail the whole way with Latrell Sprewell and Allan Houston and Jeff Van Gundy. Reggie, true to form, scored seventeen in the fourth quarter of Game 6. I know he wanted to win it at Madison Square Garden in front of Spike Lee and all the New York fans, and he got it done.

In three years, Larry Bird had taken us from the wilderness to the promised land. But in the NBA Finals, there wasn't just a coach as good as him on the other side of the court.

There were two superstars in purple and gold.

GROWING UP I had a lot of favorite athletes.

In the late '70s and early '80s, when I first got into basketball, Dr. J was one of the superstars who drew me to the sport with the Afro, the grace, the style, all the things he accomplished. A few years later, when I started thinking I was a big shot, I actually used to sign my autographs "Dr. J" You know—*J* as in *Jalen*. Maybe a little bold, but you know by now that I wasn't shy!

I also had a poster of the Iceman, George Gervin, on my wall. The Iceman was from Detroit, and had played at St. Cecilia's and Martin Luther King High School. He had a camp in the city I went to as a kid. Before the camp he would practice, which meant if you got there early you could see him finish his workout. And get this: At the end of his workout he worked on his patented shot, the finger roll—from the *free throw line*. I used to watch him make twenty-five in a row. That shot, one that looked improvised in midair, was worked on for hours at a time.

Dr. J and the Iceman were two players I was enamored with before I zeroed in on my biggest hero: Magic Johnson. Guy from Michigan, big point guard, made it big in Hollywood, he was pretty much the blueprint for me. Years later, Larry Brown would be quoted as criticizing me because I "wanted to be Magic Johnson." To which my response was "What in the world is wrong with that?"

Superstars like Magic and Larry and Michael and A.I. and the Big Ticket and LeBron and Steph are what make the NBA exciting. When players like that are at the peak of their powers, dominating play, the league is at its best. Nobody's been better at marketing their superstars than the NBA, which is what made David Stern such a great commissioner, probably the best commissioner in the history of sports. But a big part of marketing is dumbing things down, telling stories and creating images that fans can recognize and support. Magic versus Bird. Air Jordan. And so on. Most of the media discussion is on the same level. Today, more than ever, it's about simple, big questions that can be debated. Who's better—LeBron or Steph? Who was better—Jordan and the Bulls, or Magic and the Lakers? If you really know basketball, those questions don't even make any sense.

Personally, I think complicated questions are more interesting. How can Michael Jordan be both the greatest player ever ... and a guy who had a thing for gambling that got him in who-knows-what-kind-of-trouble more than once or twice? Or take my idol, Magic Johnson, one of the most marketable and appealing athletes ever ... who had to retire because he got a sexually transmitted disease. Kobe was both a basketball prodigy, one of the hardest-working players ever ... and a figure who could be a villain on the court and a man who had controversy off the court. Jason Kidd was a pass-first player who made the team game look beautiful, and made every teammate he ever played with better ... but would himself admit he's not as perfect a human being as he was a point guard.

The basketball-only stuff can be complex, too. So Shaq was a guy who couldn't win a title . . . then he was a champion when he won three with the Lakers? He may have won four titles total . . . he also was swept out of the playoffs five times. Dwyane Wade led Miami to a title, and won Finals MVP . . . he was also their top player in a season when they won fifteen games. Then we get to LeBron, the kind of player who's a cut above. Okay, so you're going to tell me he wasn't a *champion* when he was with the Cavs the first time . . . but he *was* with the Heat, when he was on a better team? Look, I was under the hoop, in attendance at the Palace at Auburn Hills, when he basically beat the Pistons by himself, scoring twenty-nine of the Cavs' last thirty points against a team that was playing in the conference finals for the fourth straight season. LeBron won two MVPs in his first stint in Cleveland. He was the best player in the league in those years. He dragged the Cavs to the Finals, the conference finals, and the playoffs every year. Just because he couldn't drag them all the way to the top was never going to take away one bit from what I thought of him.

When I was growing up, I didn't love the players everyone else did. In Detroit, the explanation wasn't just that I liked the bad guys—the Bad Boys were my team! For a few years in the middle of Magic and Bird and Michael, that Pistons team made Detroit feel like the center of the basketball world. Back in one of the golden eras of the NBA, they were champions—and they were the villains. They were another influence on my worldview at Southwestern, and on the way we approached things at Michigan.

My favorite player was the leader and the point guard of that squad, Isiah Thomas. Isiah was misunderstood for a simple reason: He went up against the guys who everyone liked. How can you beat Michael Jordan, Larry Bird, and Magic Johnson and be beloved?

Everybody's gonna hate you. In Detroit, we didn't benefit from the East Coast or the West Coast media bias. It became "Who are these thugs? These bad boys?"

If you're going to argue that Isiah stoked the fires with his actions—saying that Larry Bird would have been just another player if he weren't white, and walking off the court against the Bulls before the game was over—I'll defend him forever. These guys were *his rivals*. He was trying to *beat them*. He's not supposed to like them. He's supposed to resent them. Isiah was an important model for me in that regard. Later, I'd get to know him better when he took over for Bird as Pacers head coach. I've watched him continue to be ostracized by the media and the basketball public in the years since. All I have to say is that when you take the time to look at it from his perspective, and can peel away your biases, it makes a lot more sense. Try it sometime.

The NBA superstar who was the heir to Isiah's throne as "the outcast" was Allen Iverson. But these days, Iverson is already overlooked when people talk about the greatest NBA players. He was absolutely one of the four best players who got drafted in his era, along with Kobe, Duncan, and Garnett, yet it feels sometimes like he never played. In a lot of ways he was more influential than those guys with respect to his style, with the tattoos and the cornrows and the do-rag that were rare when he started but then became commonplace. The guy won an MVP wearing a do-rag when no one else was. When we crossed paths, A.I. would actually talk to me about how much he loved the Fab Five. If we transcended some things in college basketball, he transcended what was happening in pro basketball. The irony is the coach who got the best out of him was none other than Larry Brown, who, for at least a few years, was able to connect with Iverson and ride him to challenge the Lakers in the 2001 NBA Finals. But like Isiah and the Pistons, the Sixers in 2001 were the black hats. They were the "other guys" against the Lakers, against Kobe and Shaq, the superstar superheroes.

Superstars really are great for business. But often everything else gets pushed to the background. Including what helped create those superstars: where fate decided they'd spend their careers. For superstars, just as for the rest of us, the stars have to align.

Once they do, watch out.

WHEN YOU know the rules better than anyone, you know how to break them better than anyone. So as I tell you this story, remember that before I came clean, no one suspected anything at all.

The 2000 NBA Finals did not start well for us. The Lakers were heavily favored by everyone. They had won sixty-seven games in the regular season, had Phil Jackson on the sidelines (coming off his six titles with the Bulls), and had Shaq and Kobe playing their first year as a legendary—if tortured—tandem. This was Shaq at the peak of his powers and, sure enough, in the box score of Game 1, the thing that jumps out is forty-three points, nineteen rebounds, four assists, and three blocks from the big man. Rik Smits played twenty minutes and fouled out, and we had no one else with a prayer of stopping Shaq. As great as Shaq was in that game, Kobe was just as key in the game for L.A.

This was the Black Mamba's fourth season in the league. He was twenty-one years old, on the precipice between star and superstar. He was still in Shaq's shadow, but in reality he was already just as big a factor on that team. He had bailed them out in the seventh game of the Western Conference finals against the Blazers in that infamous collapse by Portland, and then, in Game 1, while Shaq had put up the huge numbers, Kobe had actually got them going with a fast start in the first quarter, putting them up big early. Then he played complete lockdown defense on Reggie, who finished 1-16 on the game, if you can believe that stat.

That brings us to Game 2, at the Staples Center, and me guarding Kobe as we try to turn things around. With about three minutes left in the first quarter, Kobe went up for a jumper on the wing. I turned around to look at the shot, and I felt something land on my foot. I heard a crunch, and as I ran back up the floor, I had to step over Kobe, who was suddenly curled up on the floor screaming in pain.

Oops. Casualty of war.

Now let's go back to those rules of the game. Not the ones in the book about how many timeouts you get and what constitutes illegal defense, but the rules of the game that no one ever wrote down, the ones we all learn on the street or on the playground or in pickup games in the gym. Unwritten Rule No. 1: Never stick your foot out underneath a guy after he takes a jumper. Anything could happen—a twisted ankle, a sprained foot, even a break.

Remember: The ones who know the rules best are the ones who are the best at breaking them.

I think, for better or worse, I've made clear that winning mattered to me. After all I'd gone through to get to the NBA Finals, I was there to win, not to kiss Phil Jackson's rings, or to be part of Shaq and Kobe's coronation. If you want to call me out on a dirty play, remember that my mentality was: We need to find a way to stop this guy. Countless other players like me, even superstars, have made similar moves in games of that magnitude in an effort to get the W. Like me, they knew what they were doing, and no one suspected them of being up to no good. So, yeah—I'm guilty as charged.

After we got "tangled up," Kobe limped to the sideline, and Shaq was on his own. He still managed to lead them to the win with another forty points and twenty-four boards, and some help from good games by Ron Harper and Glen Rice. But Kobe's ankle was too swollen for him to make it back for Game 3 in Indy. We made an adjustment guarding Shaq, doing more double-teams and less Hack-a-Shaq, and sure enough, we got on the board with a victory. We had two more games at home and the chance to seize control of the series. Then came the beginning of another lesson you have to consider the next time you break or bend a rule on the court.

Unwritten Rule No. 2: Karma always has the final word.

Game 4 was the best game of the series. We were up early, then they went up, then us again, then they were about to win it and ol' Sam Perkins hit a big three in the final minute to tie it and send it to overtime. That gave us the momentum, which built a few minutes into OT when Shaq fouled out. But there was still one problem: Kobe Bean Bryant. In the first of many heroic performances on his way to his five NBA titles, Kobe took control of the game and put them up two with six seconds left. Reggie missed a three to win it, and they went up 3-1 in the series. It was pretty much all she wrote from there. Yeah, we won Game 5 by thirty points, and we actually played great basketball in Game 6, but you're not going to win three straight games against Shaq, Kobe, and Phil.

Ultimately, we did everything we could against the best team in the world. As strong a team as we were, they had the three ingredi-ents of a championship team: (1) superstars—two of the greatest tal-ents of all time; (2) a legendary leader who'd already won six titles and was on his way to eleven; (3) don't forget about fate—especially after I messed with it. Kobe got karmic revenge for the foot that got stuck underneath him.

Oh, and even after taking the title, Kobe wasn't close to finished with his revenge on me.

IT WAS the greatest season of my pro career. Timing is every-thing, and it was the last year of my deal before I headed into free agency. Larry Brown had told me he'd be the one to determine if I ended up on the level of Chris and Juwan or out of the league, but actually it turned out I was going to determine that myself.

You know by now I'm not the most sentimental guy in the world, but I can't lie and claim that the thought of Jimmy Walker wasn't rattling around my head more and more that season. Coaches, assis-tants, fans, everyone was coming up to me wanting to talk about my dad, saying I looked like him, saying I played like him, saying I re-minded them of him. Yeah, I'd been hearing that for years, but now it was different. Now I wasn't trying to live up to his name. Now I'd climbed up alongside him. That letter, the one Mitch Albom had given me almost a decade earlier, was still in my house, unopened.

At some point I started carrying the envelope around in my bag, intending to open it, but not sure when. Then one day I realized the ceremony around it was overrated. I was on the team bus headed from a hotel to an arena and decided to open it, right there and then. It was just a short note that said that he had been following my progress, that he was proud of me, and that he wanted to emphasize he wasn't looking to get involved in my life just because I'd made it with the Fab Five. Mitch had tracked him down, so he felt like it was important for me to know.

A few weeks later, I was talking to my teammate Austin Croshere, who'd been a star at Providence College, where Jimmy Walker had risen to fame. After we talked about my situation, Cro' called the school's sports information office to see if they had a number for him, and—go figure—they did. By then, it was just before the playoffs, at the end of the regular season. One day I was over at Dale Davis's, where some teammates were playing poker. Poker has never been my game, so I was just hanging out, and I decided there was no time like the present. I went into D-Squared's bedroom, went into my bag, found the letter, and read it again, one more time. Then I dialed the number, and listened as the phone began to ring.

10. From the NBA Finals to a Grand Tour of Basketball's Worst Teams (and Almost Being Assassinated in Between)

A woman picked up the phone. It turned out that Austin Croshere had given me the number for Jimmy Walker's ex-girlfriend. When I explained who I was, she gave me his sister's number (technically, my aunt), who I called up right away (why stop now?). She picked up, and we started talking. I had always viewed my situation as unique, but she told me that Jimmy Walker had thirteen kids by eleven women scattered all across the country. Many of them had fallen out with him over the years, for one reason or another, and had no real relationship with their father, like me. She told me that Jimmy and his mom (technically, my grandmother) weren't getting along at the time and that was a big family problem for them. She filled me in on stuff that I didn't know anything about, and truthfully had never really thought about.

Some kids who never get to meet their dads fantasize about

where they are and what they're like. In my case, following my mom's example, I hadn't really focused on it much. No one—neither my uncles nor my family friends—had bothered thinking about him. The feeling was "out of sight, out of mind." There wasn't the time or energy to be emotional about it when we were worried about how to pay the rent and how to afford groceries. When I made that phone call, though, everything had changed. I was curious. Maybe that was because I was on the verge of having more fame and more money than Jimmy Walker ever had. I figured it was time to hear his voice.

His sister gave me yet another number, and, still sitting in Dale Davis's bedroom—I can see the paintings on the wall right now as I remember the day—I dialed again. Somebody answered the phone, I told them I was looking for Jimmy Walker, they told me to hold on, and then, *BOOM*. At age twenty-seven, I was speaking with my father for the first time.

We small-talked a little bit, and then I launched into what I wanted to tell him—that I loved him and I appreciated the fact that he was my father. That it was unfortunate we had never met, but I didn't have any hard feelings. I told him I had read the letter and, ultimately, was happy that it had led, after all these years, to us connecting. I asked him if he'd watched any of my games. He said he had, though it was clear he wasn't following me, or basketball, closely. He did share that he now played a lot of tennis, a game that I had never played—so I told him I'd love to meet him, and play tennis with him. He said great. I said maybe after the season I'll reach out, now that I've got this number, and we'll go from there. That was that. I hung up the phone, put the letter back in my bag, went back out to the living room, cracked another cold one, and got back on the couch, flipping through League Pass while the guys wrapped up the poker game.

I called him again in the off-season, after the NBA Finals were over. His number had changed again.

FOR ALL the complications of the pro life, the best and most important thing that ever happened in my NBA career was very simple. Just after midnight on the night of July 1, 2000, I got a call from the Pacers informing me that they were offering me a ridiculous amount of money to continue to play basketball for their team: $93 million over seven years. The maximum amount allowed, in fact, under the collective bargaining agreement. All guaranteed money.

Crack open some bottles!

It wasn't a surprise, but that didn't take away from the adrenaline rush. Late in the season, as we'd made our run, Donnie Walsh had let me know that I was in the team's plans, and I was going to be the first priority in the off-season, with almost every key member of the team headed toward free agency. There was going to be a lot of movement in the league—Tim Duncan, Tracy McGrady, and Grant Hill were all among a big class of free agents—but I wasn't interested in moving. I was smart enough to know I was in a good situation, and it wasn't worth messing it up by flirting with Chicago or even my hometown Pistons. So the morning after I got the call, I woke up early, went down to the team offices, and signed the deal. That was the whole thing. Nice and clean.

The transition from one season to the next was not going to be so easy. The team was in flux, starting with the corner office.

Larry Bird kept his word and resigned as head coach after three seasons. Larry wanted the job to go to Rick Carlisle, but Donnie had his mind set on a bigger splash. After seeing what Larry Bird—the proven winner, the Hall of Fame player—had done, he wanted to hire another former superstar to follow Larry—someone the players could look to and believe in. As much as I loved Carlisle, it was hard to disagree with Donnie's pick, because it was one of my idols growing up.

That said, if Carlisle had gotten the job instead of Isiah Thomas in 2000, I wonder if the second half of my career would have turned out differently.

THERE'S AN easy way to find out quick just how much the NBA is a business. Get yourself a big contract.

Growing up, I had all kinds of fantasies about getting a big deal someday. I used to dream about buying a big house with a hot tub and filling it up with forties. Do I need to confirm that I got one? I made it, and I don't regret that deal one bit.

Still, I'd be lying to you if I didn't acknowledge that getting that deal changed the course of my career from a basketball standpoint, and not necessarily in a positive way. Some of that was fate. A lot of it was business.

Isiah Thomas came to the Pacers at an interesting time. Donnie Walsh had spent a decade building a team that could reach the Finals. In its last shot, it finally did. But by then, everyone important was either at the end of their contract, or close to the end of their career. So while myself, Reggie, Cro', Travis Best, and Derrick McKey (aka "Heavy D") were brought back, other pieces were gone.

Rik Smits was thirty-three in 2000, but struggling with injuries, and he decided to retire. Mark Jackson was thirty-five, and Donnie decided to let him walk (he went to Toronto). Antonio Davis had already been dealt away for Jonathan Bender, a high school draft pick, and Donnie traded the other "Davis Brother," Dale, to Portland for Jermaine O'Neal, a former high school pick who had been languishing on the Blazers' bench. Finally, they drafted a third high schooler with high hopes, Al Harrington.

The subsequent season, 2000–2001, was a lesson in how hard it is to rebuild an NBA team. Donnie Walsh has built and rebuilt a lot of great teams in his career. In this case, he overstretched. Trying to keep both Reggie and me at high salaries while the club developed new talents around us didn't quite work as the framework of the new roster. Perhaps it would have if Larry Bird or Rick Carlisle were still there and there was a little more stability. That's the kind of stability San Antonio has had all these years with Pop while they've changed supporting casts around Tim Duncan, Tony Parker, and Manu Ginóbili. We didn't have that. In Isiah's first year, we dropped to .500, and in the first round of the playoffs we lost to Larry Brown and Allen Iverson, who were on their way to the finals.

Fast-forward to the next year, when Jermaine came into his own and made the All-Star team, and Jamaal Tinsley was a pleasant surprise as a rookie point guard. The team still played only .500 basketball, and the organization realized that it had to make a change. Everything pointed to me. First off, Reggie wasn't going anywhere, because he was an icon in Indiana. Second, I had the biggest contract, which meant moving me would give them the most return.

This was all business. The money belonged to the Pacers' owners, Herb and Mel Simon. As much as it was their prerogative to offer me the deal, it was also their prerogative to trade the deal. That was easy enough to stomach. But there's another part of a trade— what I call getting traded before you're traded. That was more difficult to take.

Think about it: How often does a trade happen when the fans don't know it's coming? When they are about to trade someone who's an integral part of a team, the organization tries to get the public's approval of a deal before it's final. If they trade a big-name player and shock the fans, they run the risk of a revolt. An NBA franchise makes money when fans come to the games and support the team. They've got to keep their fans happy.

Here's how it goes down. First, the player starts to get trashed in the media. Unnamed sources saying he doesn't practice hard, or he doesn't have the team in mind, or he parties too hard, or whatever else. The next step is lowering the player's minutes and, more specifically, keeping him out of the game in the biggest moments. Afterwards, the coach pretends it was coincidence, spouting clichés and playing it down, even though he very much did it on purpose. But it puts the idea in everyone's head—the team, the media, and the fans—that this guy is on the decline, or doesn't fit, and makes saying good-bye a lot easier, and a lot less surprising.

Check the box scores, read the old articles—it all happened to me in Indiana. It was often subtle, but it happened. I knew it was going on and what was coming. Looking back, I'm proud I handled the situation like a professional, kept coming to work, kept practicing hard, and, of course, kept cashing my checks. Though I was wrong in one aspect: I pinpointed Isiah Thomas as the culprit. Years later, I understood that, once they decided to part with their biggest contract, the organization was doing what it had to do to manage the fans and the fallout. Isiah was just the messenger. Isiah had been one of many individuals who made the decision, but he was the only one who had to execute it.

Today, I have nothing but love for Isiah Thomas and his wife, Lynn. He sponsors a classroom at the Jalen Rose Leadership Academy. We were able to patch up any gray areas. I think the reason it was so easy for us to do is that he had been a player. Eventually, I realized that while he might have been fortunate enough to spend his career with one team, he actually went through the same learning process as I did, and discovered that professional basketball needs to be thought of as a business, not just a game. If I had had that perspective when I was with the Pacers, I would have realized that Isiah is a perfect role model for players who need to understand the business aspect. During his career he was president of the National Basketball Players Association. Afterwards, he was the first player, before Michael and before Magic, to get involved in ownership, buying a stake in the Toronto Raptors and helping that franchise launch. Eventually, he ran the Continental Basketball Association, the CBA, though not so successfully. All that was before he got into coaching, and came to Indiana to replace Larry Bird.

Just a few years ago, when I was overseas with the Pacers on a preseason trip to the Philippines and Taiwan along with a few other NBA alumni, Herb Simon and I ended up talking about when he and his late brother Mel traded me. He told me that since I was the first huge deal he had ever given out, he never got comfortable with paying that much money to one player, and he was in support of dealing me. Much more than Isiah was. It was another reminder that it was just business.

All that said, in the early 2000s, I wasn't thinking about the "business." I was just wondering why they seemed to want so badly to run me out of town.

My last game was on a Sunday afternoon, at home against—of all teams—Larry Brown and the Sixers. We won, and I led the team with seventeen points, adding eight assists to boot. Two nights later, on February 19, 2002, I got the call, and hopped in my truck to drive to Chicago.

ASK ANY basketball player what his dream is, and he's supposed to immediately say: "to win an NBA title." Don't get me wrong— that's the truth. But it's not the *whole* truth.

Winning a title is great, and as a professional, it's your goal. My biggest regret is not winning a title, and not getting to be part of a championship parade. Forget the ring—I want the parade. Still, that doesn't mean it is the only thing a player works for. Fans want players who try to win a championship, and, trust me, they're working hard to do so. But they're working hard for another reason—to become an important contributor to that championship, or at least to a winning team. That's what will improve their stock around the league and will benefit them the next time they are in line for a contract. If they can string together enough years on those contracts, they can become what every NBA player truly aspires to be.

A veteran.

Why? First, a veteran is a guy who's made some real money, enough to live off for the rest of his life. But money isn't everything. Veterans are the guys who have earned something money can't buy: the respect of their peers, and the knowledge that they are a true part of professional basketball. Ask Greg Oden what he'd give to be a veteran, instead of a guy who didn't make it in the NBA after a promising college career. Switch sports and ask Tim Tebow what he'd give to be a veteran in the NFL. It's the true holy grail for all pro athletes.

Obviously, guys with a special kind of talent, like LeBron or Kobe or Jordan, are in their own category. Only a serious injury, or something totally unpredictable, would derail them from becoming a veteran. For them it's about winning titles, because titles secure legacies, or, to use the more common term, brands. For the rest of us (and almost every player eventually realizes that they're part of the larger group), becoming a veteran is in many ways the most satisfying and rewarding step in their career.

When I got to Chicago, and the Bulls had twelve wins and it was February, I knew we weren't going to run off fifteen wins in a row and somehow get back into playoff contention. If a team is bad, regardless of what fans hope for at the beginning of a season, players know they have no chance to win it all. With that knowledge, I immediately shifted my focus—from leading a Pacers team on the fringe of the playoff race to figuring out my role on a Bulls team headed nowhere. Very quickly, I realized I had to focus on being a veteran.

On championship teams, veterans are a crucial part of the equation, the keynotes right behind the coach and the superstar. Veterans keep the dynamics in the locker room in sync and the politricks under control. They are the reliable guys who know their role, and who have enough capital with their teammates to make sure everyone understands their job. Guys like Derek Fisher and Ron Harper won a lot of rings under Phil Jackson for helping keep everything in order. On losing teams, the role of veterans is just as important, because there's even more risk of guys going rogue, causing problems, and turning tough situations into really, really bad situations that don't do anyone any good.

In Chicago I became a veteran. That's why I showed up for my physical at seven in the morning the day after the trade. That's why I played in every game that season for the Bulls for a total of eighty-three games in an eighty-two-game season (Chicago had played fewer games than Indiana at the time of the deal). That's why I took guys like Eddy Curry and Tyson Chandler and Jamal Crawford under my wing, talking to them about managing their money after their rookie deals. I'd give Tyson and Eddy five hundred dollars for each double-double they got. I gave my per diem to the guys on the league minimum or ten-day contracts. Took guys out to dinner on the road. An extra role fell to me because the coach, Bill Cartwright, had an issue with his voice that prevented him from yelling at the team in practice or the huddle. As the most experienced player, I stepped in and became, in effect, the voice of the team, yelling at the team in the huddle, leading in a new kind of way for me.

To me, it also felt like a natural progression of my career and, really, my life. I had grown up in a place where mentors had played a huge role. Now, I felt like my Uncle Paramore—the one who hosted the parties, who doled out the advice, who everyone looked to as a leader. I had always acted like someone who'd grown up in the NBA, even if my connection to the league was based on the father I didn't know. Now I made good on my approach.

Maturation, though, is a lifelong process. The next season, when we were still a young, struggling team, we went back to Indiana to play the Pacers. I decided as part of my veteran duties as a leader, I was going to have a huge party at my house there for all my teammates. This party had everything—drinks, food, music, women . . . you name it. I was DJ-ing. I think it's safe to say it was the best party of the year in the NBA. Which was my goal.

Of course, we lost the next day by fifty-one points.

At twenty-nine years old, I guess the veteran game needed a little more polish.

Partying is a part of life. And a big part of the NBA life. Your workday is essentially from the late afternoon until eleven or twelve at night. After a game, you're pumped up on adrenaline and want a good meal, at least, if not also a few drinks to ease yourself off a bit. Smart players don't do this the night before a day game, but if you've got nothing the next day or night, why not? Plus, being on the road, every new city is an opportunity to sample a different kind of experience. And, yes, experience it on every level.

People ask all the time how much NBA players party. If they do drugs. If they sleep with the hottest women. My answer to that is: What do you think? Put yourself in their position. If you made a lot of money, and traveled all the time, would you go out champagning and campaigning when you had the opportunity? Yes, you would.

In your own life, do you know people who smoke weed

now and then? Of course you do. It's legal in practically half the country now. And it's no big deal. Obviously the NBA drug-tests, but especially back in my days, with one test in training camp, it wasn't rocket science to get around it. And, anyway, for offenses like marijuana and other recreational drugs, the league has a policy that allows you to get off with a warning before you get into real trouble.

With regard to women, again, if you were in the position that NBA players were, you'd find your way to some good times, absolutely.

The lesson I always tried to impart as a veteran— the most crucial component to champagning and campaigning—is not to run your mouth about it. So many guys want to talk about their exploits, talk about last night in the strip club, talk about this girl or that girl. The most successful members of basketball's social circuit, though, are the ones who operate by some rules I discovered. Never go out where people expect you to go out, and sometimes don't even go where you say you're going to go earlier in the night. And never talk about what happened last night. Be quiet about things.

IT'S A good lesson for a lot of reasons. Honestly, one of the biggest is safety. Some fans might roll their eyes, recalling stereotypes of black athletes who go to places they shouldn't be and hang out with people they shouldn't. But I am living, breathing proof (thank the Good Lord) that even when you think you're keeping yourself out of the bull's-eye, crazy things can happen. Case in point: the craziest night of my entire life.

It was September 4, 2002, six months after the trade to Chicago, and basketball history was made when superstar forward Lisa Leslie led the Los Angeles Sparks to their second straight WNBA title. Lisa had been one of the best women's basketball players in the world since she was a teenager. We came out of high school the same year, and Lisa used to date a player at USC, Lorenzo Orr, who had been a Detroit star at Pershing High, so we knew each other pretty well. Plus, our moms were friendly because they were both active in the Mothers of Professional Basketball Players (MPBP) organization.

Ever since the first summer Norm Nixon brought me out to L.A., I'd always kept a place there. I liked to spend my summers there, working out and going out. That night I was at my condo on Ocean Avenue in Santa Monica. I'd been at home playing video games with my buddy Rizz until around midnight, when we decided we'd go out for a little while. So we headed over to the Sunset Room.

Randomly, we drove over in a silver drop-top Bentley that didn't belong to me. Long story short, I'd had to take my Cadillac truck back to the dealer because it was having some wiring issues (that happens a lot when you trick out cars as much as I do), and in exchange they loaned me this Bentley, which actually belonged to Aaron Glenn, the NFL defensive back. Dealers do this from time to time. I don't know if they would have given any guy off the street Aaron Glenn's Bentley (which they were holding for him while he was out of town for a while), but for me, who they trusted to take care of it, and who they wanted to keep happy, they were willing to do it.

Anyway, back to the Sunset Room. When we walk in, who do we see but Lisa Leslie and the Sparks. Of course, we go up to them and say hi and buy them Champagne to help them celebrate. The whole time, Rizz is on me to get close to Lisa. He had it on his mind that we were gonna get together that night and make the next Kevin Garnett—the next "Big Ticket." He kept saying, "C'mon, you've got to make a little ticket tonight! You've got to make a 'ticket stub'!" No disrespect to Lisa, who is beautiful and a Hall of Famer, but Lorenzo Orr was one of my homeboys, and that was just one of the reasons neither Lisa nor I thought it was such a good idea.

Anyway, we didn't hang out for too long, because Lisa and a bunch of her teammates were leaving in the morning for a Team USA camp. We all walked out of the club together. As we got to our cars, they mentioned where they were headed, and I told them we'd lead them out to the highway because I knew a better route.

At that point, what I wasn't thinking about was that I'd already broken a few of my rules. First off, I hadn't overtipped the valet guy, which is something I always do when I go out so they keep my car right in front. Instead, I had to wait for the car for a while, standing in plain view until the Bentley was pulled up. And then, when I left, I was paying attention to the Sparks following behind me and not another red Cadillac truck that was also trailing us, which I would have noticed otherwise.

We got to the intersection of Sunset and Barrington in Bel Air and pulled up at the light. And then the red Cadillac pulled up next to me—and I saw its dome light come on. A dude sitting in the backseat of the passenger side gets out, walks over to our car, and holds up a 9 millimeter handgun.

It was completely surreal.

I couldn't hear what he said, because our window wasn't open, but it didn't matter. At that point, instinct just took over. For some reason I felt like he dropped his guard a little bit when he opened his mouth to talk. At that moment, I floored the gas and took off. I heard gunshots behind us. I ducked and kept driving, and maybe five seconds later—it felt like five minutes—I saw the I-405 come into view ahead. My escape route. I came to my senses, realized I wasn't shot, and I'm about to thank the Good Lord when—

"Yo man, I got shot!"

Rizz's face was bleeding. He's telling me he got popped in his neck, and I can see the blood, and it's crazy. We'd grown up on the west side of Detroit, and here we were in *Bel Air* and some carjacker shoots us. This was never a plotline in the *Fresh Prince*! The shot that got Rizz had thankfully gone through the headrest, but he was still bleeding—*a lot*—and it was unreal. Nothing like this had ever happened to us in the hood.

I've got one hand on Rizz's leg, trying to comfort him and tell him everything's gonna be all right, and the other hand on my cell phone as I dial 9-1-1. And I'm trying to drive because I still think these guys are chasing us. When the operator picked up, I didn't want to start screaming and get Rizz more upset, so I turned my head to the left a little bit, and talked out of the side of my mouth.

"Yeah, my dogg got shot, I want to take him to a hospital, I'm driving, could you please direct me?"

The operator gets it. She can tell the urgency in my voice, and she tells me where to go. To a hospital right off Santa Monica Boulevard.

A veterinary hospital.

I'm not kidding you.

Like I said, the hood doesn't translate well, does it?

Fortunately, almost as soon as I realized I'd taken "my dogg" to a "doggie" hospital, I looked up, and could see the sign for an actual hospital just a few blocks away.

I pulled up to the emergency room and got Rizz in there as fast as possible. They operated on him and a few hours later told me that he was going to be okay. One catch: They couldn't get the bullet out of his neck. It's still in there to this day.

They never caught the guys, either. I wasn't concerned they were targeting me specifically, so I wasn't too upset they didn't catch them. They saw a guy in a Bentley—maybe they knew it was me, maybe they didn't—who would make a good robbery target, and that's that. If I had been smarter, they never would have been able to come out of the club and follow me.

I'm not sure if the dealer cleaned up the Bentley for Aaron Glenn, or if they got him a new one. I've never caught up with him to talk about it. Maybe he knows the story, maybe he doesn't. Props to Bentley, though. That car never stopped working, even when it got hit by nine bullets.

Including one in the driver's headrest. Three inches from my head.

ALMOST GETTING assassinated wasn't the only memorable development of the spring and summer of 2002 for me. Just a few weeks before, I'd made my official debut as a member of the media, covering the NBA Finals between the Lakers and the Nets. The people at BET *MAAD Sports* had considered the offer I'd made to them at midseason—to just send a camera, and I'd handle the rest—and decided there was really nothing to lose. It had worked out pretty well. Though I was a little raw, I had the most important quality for the job: confidence.

The next year, when the Bulls missed the playoffs, I worked the Finals again, this time featuring the Spurs and the Nets. That went well, and as I started making more and more contacts, I sent around tapes of my BET coverage. *The Best Damn Sports Show Period* on Fox took notice, and I did the job at the Finals for them one year. From that gig, I became a regular correspondent on *Best Damn,* all as my playing career was continuing.

It wasn't an accident. I was a mass communications major at Michigan, and I'd always had it in the back of my head that I'd want to do TV work after my playing days were over. As my career developed, I started to look up to Jayson Williams, the former Nets forward who had begun his media career while he was still active in the league. I observed what he was doing, and kept my eyes open for opportunities to get in front of a camera. I was motivated to get better and better, especially as it became apparent that the business of basketball made it highly unlikely that I was going to be traded to a winning team before my contract ran out.

The second half of my career became a lot different from the first half. I was on playoff teams five out of my first seven years in the league. But once I got traded, I didn't sniff the playoffs again until my last season, when I was on the bench for Phoenix. Still, I continued to play at a high level, and to embrace the role of the veteran.

Where I come from, being the elder statesman doesn't necessarily mean staying quiet and following orders. Being a leader means showing your fellow players the right path, speaking up when things are messed up, and standing up when it's time to stand up. I did it in high school, I did it in college, I did it in the NBA, and I don't apologize for any of it. So, really, I'll leave it at this: the second half of my career—everything that happened after the trade from Indiana—was two things: a continuation of my favorite thing to do in the world—play basketball—and my graduate-level education for what I had decided would be my next life: telling stories from the inside on television.

ONCE I was on TV, I learned what the fans wanted. Yeah, they wanted to know why their team stank, or how it could be better, but they also wanted to know what went on behind the broadcast action.

Like the time in Indiana when we were at the height of our rivalry with the Knicks, and I'd gotten mixed up with Patrick Ewing a few times on the court. Those games were heated, and dangerous—you never knew when the talk was going to escalate into something else. The morning after a game in which we beat them in Indiana, I happened to be at the airport to pick up Rizz when I came across all the Knicks' luggage in the terminal, stacked where the team planes took off. I happened to see one box—a trunk, really—with a sticker that said "Patrick Ewing" on it. I happened to shuffle over to the trunk, get it open, and discover it was a TV/VCR combo, also labeled with his name.

In the NBA at that time, star players like Patrick Ewing would sometimes get their own TVs so they could watch game tape on the road. Well, Patrick was nowhere to be seen. The Knicks probably hadn't even gotten to the airport yet; their luggage had probably been sent ahead. Since Rizz was around to help me carry it, I figured I'd be opportunistic, and help myself to the TV. I was just looking for a little competitive advantage, west Detroit style. I kept that TV for years in my house, and the sticker that said "Patrick Ewing" never came off. Meanwhile, Patrick claims he never knew it was missing. But Jeff Van Gundy corroborated my story—he was coaching the Knicks, and they had to buy Patrick a new one.

Another night was an example of the bling-bling in the league, a trend that I was definitely a part of. (Remember my bracelet—"the Mansion"?) Players would regularly bring a heap of jewelry on the road, and during games we gave it to the trainer to hold, or put it in an envelope, wrapped tape around it, and left it in our bags. Not the most genius idea. One night in Milwaukee, my jewelry got stolen out of the locker room during the game. Everybody else had theirs, but mine had disappeared. I didn't care if the bus was waiting—I wasn't going to leave town without finding my stuff. They made everyone who was still working at the arena get frisked. My stuff didn't turn up, and we left, but the aggressive approach worked. Whoever stole it must have gotten scared and thrown the loot under the bleachers. When I got home I was told some cleaning people had found it, and I sent Rizz from Indiana back to Milwaukee to claim it.

That was a bad night. Truth is, there were a lot of disappointing nights after I got traded to the Bulls. In Chicago, while I embraced the role of being a veteran on a losing team, and played well, leading the team in scoring, I couldn't escape the politricks.

The 2002–2003 Bulls team—my first full season in Chicago—achieved some infamy a few years back when Jay Williams talked about players always being high, even on the bench during games. In the interest of getting things on the record, please know that I'm shaking my head right now. I'm not going to tell you that no one on that team ever smoked weed, but not during games.

Jay was in a tough situation that year. He had been drafted to be a savior, to take Jamal Crawford's backcourt position after Jamal hurt his knee. Jay and Jamal naturally clashed, and Jay felt like I was on Jamal's side, because of our Michigan connection. The next thing you know, there were leaks about me breaking off plays and not listening to coaches. I don't think Jay leaked those stories, but when players get frustrated, they talk to their boys and their agents and their friends, and those people talk to people, and that's how the politricks work.

Despite all that, I was the one who hung Jay's jersey in our locker room after his motorcycle accident. Before that, I was one of the people who told Jay to get rid of that bike. Now we're both at ESPN, and we've done the McDonald's All-American game together and had a blast with it. We're all good.

With the Toronto Raptors, where I got dealt early in the 2003–2004 season, my luck wasn't any better, and the politricks got even worse. In mid-February, we were playing against the Golden State Warriors one night, still in the playoff hunt, when I broke the fourth metacarpal on my left hand (I'm left-handed) trying to swipe the ball away from Clifford Robinson. I ended up missing more than a month after the surgery. By the time I returned, the Raptors were out of contention. Though I'm proud of one thing: I finished the game that night. I remember telling Donyell Marshall, our forward, to throw the ball to my right hand, not my left, when he passed it to me. When our coach, Kevin O'Neill, who I was a big fan of, found out I needed surgery, he broke a lamp in his hotel room and got into trouble with the team. Maybe he knew what was coming—he ended up getting fired at the end of the season.

Now for the politricks in Toronto. They really didn't involve me so much as the Raptors' superstar-in-residence, Vince Carter. Vince was the second most gifted talent I've ever played with, behind Chris Webber. His gifts were simply amazing: His athleticism was off the charts (he's the only guy I ever saw do a full-360 dunk in a game), he could shoot, and he was a good dude. He had taken an expansion franchise that had never won anything and, within a year of his arrival, had led them to the postseason. By the time I got there, though, the bottom had dropped out. The team hadn't built well around him, and the franchise's response was to dump on him. There'd be stories in the media about Vince, questioning his injuries and his durability (funny—he's still playing more than a decade later), talking about his mom and where she parked her car, all kinds of stuff that was leaked from inside the organization.

It came to a head one night in 2004 when Sam Mitchell, the coach of a new regime that came to the Raptors espousing a "new philosophy" (funny how many new philosophies come and go in the NBA), had words with Vince while he was on the training table before a game in Portland. One thing led to another, and next thing you know, they're wrestling. Then Vince lifts old Sam up and body-slams him on the ground. I've told the story before, and Sam has denied it, but what else is he going to do? This happened, I was there, and so was almost the entire team.

Bill Simmons and other guys get on me for defending Vince, but

I saw it from the inside. I saw a guy who was committed to his franchise and got hung out to dry, and then, about a month after the incident with Sam Mitchell, Vince was traded. And you know that the franchise didn't know what they were doing with that deal because of what happened with one of the guys Vince was traded for—Alonzo Mourning. Zo had no interest in coming to Toronto and a losing team, which led to a sticky situation. The Raptors thought they could convince him to play in Toronto, which wasn't going to happen, and they ended up having to buy him out. A year later, Zo had an NBA title with Pat Riley and the Miami Heat.

Meanwhile, for me, the 2005–2006 season had some crazy twists and turns—starting with a night in Los Angeles, when you might say Kobe Bryant got his ultimate revenge on me for the Finals a few years earlier.

Phil Jackson was back with the Lakers after his hiatus, and since Kobe was all the Lakers had, he was a scoring machine that year. Sam Mitchell had the idea to defend him with a 1-2-2 zone, and it kind of worked in the first half. Kobe had 26 points, but we were up 14. After halftime, the Black Mamba decided he wasn't going to lose to the last-place Raptors and went to work like arguably no one in the history of the NBA. He scored 55 on us in the second half—it almost sounds impossible—to finish with an immortal 81 points. Only Wilt scored more, in his famous 100-point night. We were on our way to a twenty-seven-win season, so it wasn't LeBron scoring 45 points against the Celtics in Game 6 of the conference finals. It wasn't even as impressive as when Kobe had scored 62 points against the Mavs a month earlier, a team that would make the NBA Finals. Still, I don't think anyone will ever approach that number. A handful of guys in the league are capable of putting up 60 on any given night, but I don't know if we'll see 81 again.

Kobe didn't say a word that night. Not one word. But way in the back of my head, the voice I heard was simple.

This is basketball karma. This is what you get—even five years later—when you mess with Kobe Bryant.

THAT SEASON, my contract was a year from expiring. Toronto wanted to deal me, and this time, they didn't want to get burned doing it. And who was interested but the New York Knicks, whose general manager was none other than Isiah Thomas, and whose coach was none other than, yes, Larry Brown. It was as surprising to me then as it is now, but the word was that as Larry was trying to remake the Knicks during a disastrous season at Madison Square Garden, he thought I would be a good addition. The man who helped broker the deal was William Wesley, aka World Wide Wes. Today, he's well known for his connections all across the game, functioning as an uncle to many guys in the league, and a consultant for the Creative Artists Agency (CAA). Then he was more in the shadows, helping to squash the beef between me and Larry. Wes knew both of us well and worked to get us to get over what was between us.

As the rumors about me coming to the Knicks were flying, I got on the phone with Larry. He said he regretted what had happened in Indy, and it would be different in New York. I appreciated that. I also talked to Isiah, who gave me a lot of love, too. I said, "Great, I'm in, I'd be happy to play for you," and I got traded for Antonio Davis.

(The second time in my career I got traded for Antonio. He was also a former teammate.)

Two days later, I picked up the paper in New York, and Larry was quoted as saying he didn't want me there. It was the same old Larry Brown—the guy who loves everybody who's not on his team, but then once he gets them, he doesn't want them. Apparently that went for guys that had even been on his team previously, like me. Larry's like the guy who wants to date every girl, but once he gets them, he can't stand them anymore. I was furious, but I was stuck.

The Knicks were the third losing team I'd be on since Indiana, and without question, they had the most dysfunctional locker room. We talk a lot on the podcasts about the "Keep Cashing Dem Checks" All-Stars, guys who strike gold with a huge contract, even though the most significant thing they do during the contracts is cash their checks, and the "All-Velvet-Rope" All-Stars, guys who do their best work at the clubs late at night. The Knicks' roster was full of both.

Larry had a five-year contract worth more than $50 million, which he saw as bulletproof protection from getting fired, and a crazy strategy. He was going to tear down this team and show everyone how he could build it back up the next year. The process was so ugly—between Larry and Isiah, and Larry and the Knicks' owner, Jim Dolan—that the Knicks did end up firing him. They paid him almost $20 million in severance. I'm sure Larry had no problem cashing that check.

Fortunately, after the season, Isiah played me fair and worked out a buyout with my agents for the last year of my deal, leaving me free to sign with any team I wanted. And with a choice of some contending teams who were looking for a veteran to help them out, I picked Phoenix, which in retrospect was a mistake. If I could do it over, I'd pick Miami, where I would have played for an all-time great, Pat Riley. Instead, I barely played with the Suns. With my media career becoming more and more the focus, I retired from playing after the 2006–2007 season.

At some point that year, I came to the realization that it finally was time to meet my dad in person. We'd probably spoken three or four times since that initial phone call in 2000. He'd popped in and out of my head over the years—when I became a father, in 2001, and a few years later in Toronto, when I passed him on the all-time scoring list. Together, we'd become the all-time father-and-son scoring tandem in NBA history, which was a cool thing to share. (Sorry, Kobe and Jellybean Bryant—you're not going to get me on this one; I'm only counting guys with 10,000 points or more.) Sometime in the spring of 2007, I tracked him down in Kansas City and made a loose plan to come there after the season.

But in the beginning of July, right after I'd worked the Finals for Fox, I got a call from Dave Bing. Did you hear the news? he wanted to know. I hadn't.

Jimmy Walker had died. He was sixty-three years old.

JALEN'S ALL-TIME CHAMPAGNING AND CAMPAIGNING HALL OF FAME STARTING FIVE

(Simple Rules and Criteria: Must be retired—no active players—and must be in their respective Halls of Fame, or headed there, to be eligible for this honor.)

G ALLEN IVERSON

Subject of countless urban legends. Made cornrows fashionable. Almost single-handedly responsible for David Stern's instituting a dress code.

QB "BROADWAY" JOE NAMATH

Wore a fur coat on the sideline. Guaranteed a Super Bowl. Epitomized cool.

F CHARLES BARKLEY

Every team needs an enforcer. Once threw a heckler through a glass window. Never a role model. Always made any party better.

CB DEION SANDERS

"Prime Time." "Neon Deion." Godfather of high stepping. Took a limousine to the NFL Scouting Combine, then ran a 4.19-second forty-yard dash. Urbanlegendly, that is.

F DOMINIQUE WILKINS

"The Human Highlight Film." "The Chocolate Boy Wonder." His exploits off the court went under the radar. His high-top fade did not.

FOURTH QUARTER

Press Pass

11. From BET to ESPN and All Points in Between, or Why Chris Webber and I Haven't Spoken in Five Years

Two months after the end of my NBA career, I finally met my father.

I didn't feel sad. I didn't feel angry. I didn't feel numb. All I felt was fear, fear brought on by seeing so few people at a memorial service for a sixty-three-year-old man. I'm not sure what the temperature was that summer day in Kansas City, but that was the coldest room I've ever been in.

Jimmy Walker had thirteen kids (that people knew of). Besides me, only two others showed up to pay their respects.

He'd made hundreds of friends in a great basketball career. Almost none of them had come to see him off.

The man who had unknowingly, but undeniably, set my course in life, left this world, and hardly anybody wanted to say good-bye to him.

When I got there, I had expected to see the body resting in a coffin—to lay eyes on him for the first time. Instead, he had been cremated, and all that was there was an urn with his remains. So that day I would have to settle for meeting my father through the speakers at the service. They each represented a different stage of his life and career. A woman named Gail Silva, who had been a longtime girlfriend and friend, talked about his days at Providence. Dave Bing waxed poetic about his time with the Pistons. And Darryl Mays talked about where he ended up, in Kansas City with the Kings. Years later, though, I can't really recall one word of what they said. To me, the coldness of the room overpowered everything.

Up to that moment, having Jimmy Walker as someone to compare myself to had been a positive thing. He was an NBA player, so I was going to be an NBA player. He was an All-Star, so I was going to be an All-Star. I had parted long ago with any bitterness or hostility. I was appreciative of how great a player he was. All told, he was better than me.

Now that he was dead, I could see what he'd left behind, and fear replaced the sense of admiration. I realized that day that in my life I had to do everything I could to end up as far away as possible from that cold, half-empty funeral home.

That day I determined to become a better man, a better role model, and, yes, a better father. I was also thinking about all the professional goals I still had. I had already decided I wasn't going to spend the rest of my days just sitting on a beach somewhere. At that point, it would have been easy to congratulate myself on kick-starting my television work while I was a player, and to settle for a spot on a standard show, phone in the work, and collect my paycheck. But that wasn't me. That wasn't the best I could do.

Since that day, I've always approached my second career with the same sense of competitiveness I took to the basketball court. I want to be better than my NBA peers who became part of the media when their careers ended. I want to do more than just be on a show. I want to have a multimedia presence on as many platforms as possible. I want to have the most Twitter followers. I want to win an Emmy. Really, it's all about being a professional at the highest level of my field.

It took me ten years to get myself to the top levels of the media business: to being a lead studio analyst on ESPN, to a prominent place on *Grantland*, and to the point where someone would pay me money to write a book. As the great Parrish Smith put it—"no shorts and no sleep," right?

People ask me why I always have a baseball bat resting on my shoulder in my *Grantland* podcast videos. The bat on my shoulder represents the chip on my shoulder, the same chip I carried around as a player at Southwestern, at Michigan, and in the pros. I've transferred it to media. People are surprised that *I'm* the lead studio analyst for ESPN? That *I'm* calling games in college and the pros, and all over *Grantland*? Perfect. That just feeds the chip. And my bat and I are just getting started.

I've had plenty of time, as a player and as a member of the press, to figure out not just how media and fans misunderstand sports, but why.

So now it's my job to help set everybody straight.

We get tricked into thinking that sports are a fantasyland, a magical place with a magical set of standards and practices. That the crazy-rich players should be happy with the money they get from their crazy-rich owners. That everybody should listen to their coach and fall in line behind the front office, no matter what.

Within this fantasy frame of mind, when LeBron James moves from Cleveland to Miami, the story line is that he "abandoned" the Cavaliers. When Carmelo Anthony decides not to go to Chicago but stay in New York, he "doesn't care about winning" and is just "all about the money." When a player like Dwight Howard, or back in my day, Vince Carter, starts having problems with his organization and forces a trade, he's turning his back on his teammates.

That is the way those stories are depicted. And most fans believe the narrative the media, and the owners, spin for them. But the magical pedestals we put our sports figures on—and the values we assign to their moves— aren't grounded in reality.

Let me ask you a few questions. If you got a job offer for a better job at a better company, would you take it? If you had a chance to get a raise, would you take it? If your company was poorly run, and clearly headed nowhere good, would you speak up or look for a new job? If you're the best at what you do in your field, you become a commodity. You have options about where you work and where you live.

In sports, for some reason, we don't expect the athletes

to act like everyone else does in relation to their jobs. People who follow sports should make more of an effort to see an athlete's actions from the athlete's perspective.

Flipping to the other side of the equation, there's the game that pro athletes have to play with the media. Many of those athletes could learn how to manage their reputations a little better. LeBron and "the Decision" is a cardinal example of how not to play the game. LeBron said so himself when he returned to Cleveland. (That return, by the way, was the cardinal example of how to do things.) The problem was never that he went to Miami, a better organization at the time, with an iconic leader ready to guide him to the promised land. The problem was how he went about it, and that's on him.

The central rule here is pretty simple: You have to win first, and build the image second. Now that LeBron's won titles, no one can criticize him in quite the same way they once did. To take another example, go back to Vince Carter. You might remember that situation a few years ago with him in Game 7 of the conference semis against the Sixers. He went to graduation at North Carolina in the morning and flew back just in time for the game, which his team lost by a point. There were a lot of people who found what Vince did that day admirable. There were also a lot of haters, who thought of him as soft for not prioritizing winning over everything else. If Vince had *asked me for my advice, I would have told him not to go. As significant as it was to graduate from college, at that moment it was more important to do his job and build the case that he was a superstar. He had a lot more great games in him—he still might—but he never reached a higher plateau in his career than on that day.*

He should have won first, and found a time to walk later.

ULTIMATELY, WHAT winning gets you is something I call "media equity." It's an imaginary pass that entitles you to "benefit of the doubt" treatment from most people covering the sport. In today's game, Kobe, LeBron, D-Wade, and Dirk Nowitzki are examples of superstars who've earned equity by taking home titles. But there are other ways to get it, incredibly simple ways. Like just being nice to a lot of writers and broadcasters. Giving them thoughtful quotes (even if they're not always truthful). Complimenting them if you think they wrote a good column. Saying hi to them and being courteous. A ton of coaches are great at this. Mike D'Antoni would hold open practices in Phoenix to give the media the sense they were getting cool access. Doc Rivers was in the media before coaching and understands how to play the game. Gregg Popovich does, too. How else do you think he gets away with all those grouchy in-game interviews?

Lots of players get it as well. Shaq was a master, acting like a class clown who the media loved. A couple of guys you might not expect—Allen Iverson in Philly and Tim Duncan in San Antonio—

have always gotten great treatment in their markets. There's a reason for that. There's nothing shady about it. They just know how to play a pretty simple game quite well.

Other guys take a while to get used to the media weighing in on their situations. Dwight Howard had a rough time in his one season in Los Angeles a few years ago. He even got on me when I said the Lakers should trade him. Then, when we spoke about it, I reminded him that he left the team in free agency—so they should have traded him! We both laughed, and moved on.

For me, dealing with little brushfires like that is a hazard of the media trade. Because of course, every night on ESPN, and on every podcast on *Grantland*, my job is to give my honest opinions, and those opinions aren't always positive. At other times, I drop a line like "Hey, this player might go here" or "Watch out for this team looking to make this kind of deal," and it starts a little media forest fire with everyone else running to that team or player asking for comment. The best part of my job is accumulating a ton of information. One of the toughest parts is choosing what to say on the air.

Because whether it's on the record or off the record, the best way to think of NBA media—and sports media at large—is to consider it a giant information exchange. When I wake up in the morning, when I go to sleep at night, and when I'm on the air I get texts and calls from different people around the league feeding me information. Players, coaches, GMs, agents, entourage members, you name it. Sometimes they're calling to give their side of a story. Sometimes they're calling to get something out of me. A GM will call me up and throw out a little air balloon—"Hey, what do you think of So-and-So as a player? What do you hear about him?"—hoping for some insight into how it'll be perceived if they sign him. They don't always tell me to keep something secret; it's understood that I'll know what to say and what not to say. Sometimes they want me to say something on air. Remember, the first step to trading a player is to trade him in the media and let your fans know what might be coming. In a lot of cases, it's an exchange. They need me as much as I need them.

For a reporter who's never played the game, who starts at a newspaper or a website, it takes years to build those kinds of sources. I had them from the get-go, because they were literally hundreds of individuals I knew from more than a decade in the NBA. Overall, I've kept pretty much every friend I started with, so I feel that I'm doing a good job of knowing what to say and what not to say, and how to do the job.

But there is one friendship that's on hold right now.

IT'S BEEN a long climb up the media mountain. *Best Damn Sports Show* was a really great show to cut my teeth on, because they were up for almost any idea we had. I did all kinds of crazy little features, sideline work at games, red carpets, big events, you name it. As I got experience, I was able to improve and get more comfortable. As I continued my media career, I learned to use my contacts and connections to get what other reporters couldn't. Like at the 2006 Finals, when a PR guy—on air—tried to move me out of the way when Dwyane Wade walked by. Instead, I was able to get close to D-Wade, and we ended up walking down the tunnel getting the interview right then and there. And I also had a lot of fun with celebrities, interviewing Denzel Washington and Penny Marshall, and even Jack Nicholson once. And nobody interviews Jack, ever. Except for me, I guess.

When I got hired by ESPN in 2007, I moved over to the studio, appearing on all different shows, spending a lot of time in Bristol, Connecticut, paying my dues. Also, I was getting better. I did as much moonlighting as I could, hosting live events like weigh-ins for big fights, and even a little acting. C'mon, you don't remember my cameo interviewing Common in *Just Wright*? Of course you do.

As I built up more and more cred at ESPN, I started pursuing my dream project: a documentary on the Fab Five. I wanted a chance to tell our story the way we wanted to, the way it hadn't been told at the time. When ESPN got their *30 for 30* series going, it seemed like our story would be a perfect fit. In 2010, the higher-ups green-lighted the film with me as executive producer. The idea was pretty simple: Jimmy, Ray, Juwan, Chris, and I would tell our tale, the good, the bad, and the ugly. Almost twenty years after the fact, we'd have the official record of the Fab Five on film forever. But pretty quickly, I realized we might have a problem. Chris wasn't returning my texts or calls about setting up our interviews.

A lot had happened to both of us since we'd walked off the court in New Orleans in the 1993 national title game. While I had been doing my thing, Chris had had a terrific NBA career, probably a Hall of Fame career, if I had a vote. He was a former Rookie of the Year, a five-time All-Star, and had played for the Warriors, and then the Bullets (alongside Juwan), and then the Kings, leading all those teams to the playoffs. He led the Kings to the best record in the league in 2002. Unfortunately, they came up short in infamous fashion, losing to the Lakers in the conference finals, which was marred by Tim Donaghy and a bunch of very controversial calls.

Chris had bad luck with injuries, too. He struggled with nagging problems in the early part of his career and suffered a devastating knee injury that eventually led to microfracture surgery, which compromised his game for his last several years in the league. He played pretty well for our hometown Pistons in 2007, though they were the team that LeBron basically beat single-handedly with the Cavs in the conference finals. To everyone else, that series was about how amazing LeBron was. To me, it was a reminder of how little is guaranteed in basketball. It felt like just a minute earlier, Chris had been LeBron, the guy who everyone couldn't wait to see dominate the league.

Alongside the game, there was our relationship, and C-Webb's relationship with all of us. In Michigan, while the rest of us were basically bonded at the hip, Chris had always been, like, "I'm with you all, but I have my other friends, too." We always respected that, but it could lead to some surprises. One example: I drove down to Freaknik in Atlanta with Ray and Jimmy. When we got there, we were surprised to see Chris there with some other guys. That wouldn't have happened with any other member of the Fab Five. When he left school, the rest of us played another year together, so that distanced him a little further from the group.

Once I went to the NBA, anytime our teams played each other, Chris and I would get together to have a few drinks and do it up like the Fab Five used to, especially in those early days when both Chris and Juwan were in Washington. But, over time, Chris's relationship with us got more and more distant. The same thing happened to you, too, with high school or college friends, I'm sure. Little things change—like Chris started not calling people back. Or I'd hear from Ray that Chris had a game in San Antonio and said he'd leave tickets for Ray (who settled in Austin after college), but when Ray got to will-call, nothing was there, and there was no one to contact. It happened to me, too. There was an All-Star Game in Cleveland—my first season in Indy, when Larry Brown was keeping me out of the lineup, and Chris was in Washington. He had made the All-Star team for the first time, and he invited a few of the old crew to come out and support him. So a couple of our boys from Detroit, Tim and Kev, and I went to Cleveland, and to the hotel where he said he'd make sure we had rooms arranged (I was going to pay—but rooms are hard to get over All-Star weekend on late notice). Well, guess what? No rooms. So we ended up having to drive around for two hours, and eventually got rooms way out in the suburbs. Not the end of the world, but for me, it was a reality check as to what the relationship had become.

Those are a few of the examples of what we had to deal with as a family. I'm not trying to be petty—I've talked about many of these things at one point or another before. I'm just keeping it 100, and telling you what's happened, and doing it for a specific reason.

Anyway, all that stuff was still bubbling beneath the surface when the 2009 Final Four came to Ford Field, where the Lions play, in Detroit. Michigan State had made it to the title game, and Jimmy had the idea to use the opportunity to have a Fab Five reunion. I got on board. We wanted to show the college basketball world that we weren't erased from history, even if our banners weren't hanging up in Ann Arbor. Our idea was to get some publicity behind it, have a few parties and engagements, and then sit courtside at the game. For us to be in the spotlight, in prime seating, at a big-time event with one of our archrivals playing—it felt like a fitting thing for the Fab Five to do. So we started getting things together. Buying tickets on the court, doing work, all that. Only then we get word—Chris wasn't gonna show. No reunion. No family.

That brings us back to the documentary a couple years after that. Which, as you probably know, Chris decided he wasn't going to be a part of. We of course went ahead and did it without him, even though that meant we didn't get the ending I wanted: all five of us chilling together, on a balcony at the Gansevoort hotel in New York, with a lobster buffet out in front of us, almost mafioso style, showing how we clearly won the game of life, regardless of what happened in those title games. Well, even without that ending it became the highest-rated doc in the history of the network at the time. People still come up to me almost every day with something to say about it. I'd like to think it squared our legacy away for good. Though of course, in the process, it pretty much put my relationship with Chris on ice.

That's my side of it. His side of it, as far as I can tell, is a couple of things. One, obviously, he didn't want to do the doc, even though I'd gotten a buy-in from him before I pitched it to ESPN. I guess he decided he didn't want to talk about the timeout, or what happened with the grand jury. But the question I have is, why did Chris go for a meeting with Ross Greenburg and HBO Sports, after we'd already started our project, to undercut ours and get his own Fab Five documentary going? And what's he doing now with a documentary apparently in the works as I write this in 2015? Did he not like the fact that I was producing it at ESPN? All of us were going to be producers. If you watch the film, we're all equally featured, and everyone gets their say. Maybe he felt like the doc should have been about him only. I guess we'll have to wait for his documentary and see.

In the meantime, let's go back to Ed Martin. Yeah, that's still going on in 2015. The punishments that Michigan received for the scandal included a ten-year "mandatory disassociation period" between Chris and the school. (If you could tell me the point of that, I'd love to hear it, but I'm done complaining about the NCAA at this point.) In 2013, that period was due to expire, so a lot of questions were coming up. Like, if they did "reconcile," could there be a Fab Five reunion at the school? I always thought the best thing to do would be to just put a new banner up, with "Fab Five" on it and our numbers, and hang it on a night to remember with all of our friends and families and fans, and that would be that. Well, it became clear that Mary Sue Coleman, then the president of the university, made it clear that the banners weren't going up on her watch. And Dave Brandon, then the athletic director, made it clear that, in his mind, the school was going to need a formal apology from Chris for anything close to that to happen anyway.

I spoke out about President Coleman's remarks quite loudly on Twitter, but as far as the apology went, when people started asking me about it, I said that if it were me, I would apologize. Why? At some point, you need to accept responsibility for whatever you did, even if you think you were wronged, and move on. Owning it, speaking about it—that helps you get over it. Plus, it would give everyone a path forward to restoring the legacy of the Fab Five at Michigan. At this point, I feel like the rest of us are kids in the middle of a fight with their parents. But in this case, there's no reason why they shouldn't clear the air on both sides and reconcile. And maybe that could start with an apology.

Well, Chris didn't like that I said that, and that's led to some weird, ugly exchanges over the last few years. In the spring of 2013, when Michigan made it to its first title game since our day, I tried again to get us all together, let bygones be bygones with Chris, and go to the game and sit together. I talked about it on my podcast, went public with my request, but it didn't work. Chris actually went to the game but sat upstairs while the other four of us were down below. Then, a few months later, at the NBA Finals, our ESPN studio set was just a few feet from the Turner set, where he was working. We had been through a similar scenario the previous few Finals, and had done a pretty good job of avoiding each other. On this afternoon, after we'd taped some things, I was with Bill Simmons. Bill and I had been spending a ton of time together on the road, he had heard all these stories, and he couldn't believe everything I had been telling him was true—that there was this much animosity about something that could be easily squashed. Bill was egging me on to walk over to the Turner set, and so we did. We said hi to each guy on the set, and when I got to Chris he told me in five words or less—using stronger language than this—to get out of his face. I did. Then, that night at the clubs, I had the luck of running into him at Liv, and we had a few words. He mentioned the apology thing in the midst of another rant telling me to go somewhere else. Dale Davis, who'd played with me in Indiana, and with Chris in Detroit, was standing right there, kind of caught in the middle of it. I wasn't going to go to start having it out with him at the club, so I just walked away rather than get in his face. That shouldn't be our flavor, anyway, certainly not between two professional adults, let alone two brothers who aren't getting along.

Let's go through what's happened since Chris Webber and I first played basketball together at age thirteen. We went to Michigan together and were part of a team that will never be forgotten. We both had long and successful pro careers. We both are having successful careers in the media. But in the game of life, relationships are most important. The Fab Five showed that to me as much as anything else. Other than that national title game against Louisville in 2013—with him sitting in a suite, us in the stands, on the opposite end of the arena—it's been twenty years since the members of the Fab Five have been together in one place. And, ultimately, that's just ridiculous.

Chris and I are both winning the game of life. He had a great NBA career, and he's having a great career at TNT. And just like me—and just like anyone—he's made some mistakes along the way. Fine. But it's not right that the brotherhood has been fractured. It bothers me. It's why I'm writing about it—not to sound like a jilted lover, not to reveal some secret gossip—but because it's not right. Everything that shaped our lives happened to us together. We won as brothers, we lost as brothers. And as his brother, I think that if he owned the things that have gone wrong—namely, the timeout and the grand jury—then he would be better off. Forgetting and letting negative things out of your heart cure the soul.

Only time will tell if Mayce Edward Christopher Webber III realizes that.

WELL, LET'S talk about the future, the future of basketball. I am a huge fan of pretty much every sport you can think of, and maybe a few you couldn't, but if you gave me a pot of money to bet on the prospects of one sport, I would put my money on the hardwood without fail.

Right now, the league is in tremendous shape. David Stern was bar-none the best commissioner of any game in the history of sports. If you think of what the NBA was when he started, and where it is now, the comparisons end. Yes, the league was rising when he came in on the wings of Magic and Bird and then Jordan, but the vision to globalize was David Stern's. He was the one who saw what could happen with the 1992 Dream Team, and the influence that team could have. Fast-forward twenty-plus years and basketball is right alongside soccer as the world's game. That's transformed the league for the better. The foreign players that started to flood the NBA in the second half of my career are more prevalent than ever. Also, you might note, more diverse. The trip to Taiwan and the Philippines with the Pacers and Rockets I told you about opened my eyes to how popular the NBA and the game are far beyond the hood and the playground in the United States.

Now Adam Silver has taken over as NBA commissioner, and he's probably open to a few more changes than Stern was, which is a good thing. You want to be flexible and willing to adapt: creating a longer All-Star break; changing up the playoffs a bit; and whatever else he has up his sleeve to make what's already good, great. The new head of the players union, Michele Roberts, isn't going to give him any breaks, but I'm hopeful that continued success leads to a reluctance to tolerate any more work stoppages when the next agreement is likely negotiated in 2017.

In terms of quality of play, the league is better than ever. Guys are bigger, they're faster, and they're stronger. In football, that makes the game more dangerous. In basketball, it makes it more exciting, and more unbelievable when you see what these guys can do. I always shake my head when people start trying to make all these intergenerational comparisons—is LeBron better than Oscar Robertson, or is Chris Paul better than Bob Cousy. It is simply a different game played today. The questions about who's better are the wrong questions to ask.

Today, guys are expected to be able to do everything. Magic Johnson was one of the most versatile players ever, right? He was a point guard, but also started at center in the 1980 NBA Finals. Well, in 1982–83, Magic Johnson didn't make one three-pointer the whole season. Altogether, his team made ten all season. Ten. There are guys in the league who regularly hit ten a week now on their own. That's how much the game has changed. Also, when I came up, the runners and floaters that I threw up were considered to be wild, wacky, low-percentage shots. Well, today, with more athletic defenders, you have to be able to hit those. Look at guys like D-Wade, Derrick Rose, and Tony Parker, who find ways to hit all kinds of shots. Players today have better nutrition plans and training methods with hyperbaric chambers and full-body ice machines. In the NBA's dirty little secret, they also have access to human growth hormone and steroids that lurk around the league as well. That makes them better, no doubt, and, unlike baseball, the public doesn't seem to care, at least for the time being.

There's another sign of success: the ever-skyrocketing value of franchises. What we're talking about is a business, right? If the franchises are selling, that means the marketplace sees something in the game. Over the last few years, teams that have never won a championship are selling for two and three times what they were bought for not so long before. That's because a lot of these teams can flourish and be the most popular teams in their cities without necessarily winning titles. If more than a dozen of the NBA franchises made it to the second round of the playoffs, their fans would want to have a parade for them. I'm not saying the management or the owners don't want to win a title. I'm just saying that a winning season with a playoff victory would be viewed as a huge, and very profitable, success. That's a good place for a league to be in. Plus it's also very possible for a lot of teams to make it into the conference semis, since eight teams—almost a third of the league—do.

In other words, the system works.

FOOTBALL AND baseball—America's other two "big sports"—are also phenomenally successful right now from a business stand-point. But they have problems now, and on the horizon, that they're going to have to deal with. With football, it's the danger issue. As I said, better and stronger athletes in football mean harder hits and more dangerous plays. A lot of people worry about a guy dying right on the field. Personally, as a former childhood player, and a huge fan (Go, Lions!), I love the violent aspect of the game, and I know the players love it, too. But you can't ignore the costs. Now that the public is more and more aware of those costs, the league is starting to legislate the violence out of the game, which for a lot of fans is its most appealing part. In basketball, the better and stron-ger the athletes are, the more amazing the plays are going to be.

Baseball is still successful. Even if its national TV ratings aren't as high as the NFL's or the NBA's, attendance and local TV contracts make all those franchises billions of dollars. But the sport has got its issues—first and foremost, steroids and performance-enhancing drugs. Most fans have an issue with the drugs because they put the stats out of whack, and that impacts the record book, which is like the Holy Bible of baseball. Actually, a bigger issue is that young kids in a high school are taking the drugs to perform, not doing it safely, and killing themselves. That's a problem, and it's a tragedy. I under-stand why the pros do it, I really do. But they have to find a way to keep it out of the high school game. Concerning drugs in basketball, yeah, I see their presence in the college and pro games. Get back to me when we start seeing evidence of it impacting the health of kids.

Baseball's still fiddling with their playoff system, trying to make it fair, and always pissing someone off. They're still figuring out instant replay. Also, what's with the managers wearing uniforms? Old dudes with the tight pants—they've got to cut that out. But seriously, baseball has another long-term problem the NBA doesn't: race. Baseball was where Jackie Robinson, Willie Mays, and Hank Aaron became American heroes. Now fewer than 10 percent of major league players are African American, and that number's sinking. No, I'm not claiming that blacks are better athletes than whites. But I do think that blacks and whites approach sports (and entertainment) completely differently. For white kids living in the cul-de-sacs, sports are a hobby. For black kids in the hood, it's the only way out.

Race is a central part of any discussion about the future of sports, because for a long time, sports have been the central way that our country experiences race. Athletes like LeBron James and Kevin Durant are some of the first black people that white kids in the suburbs get to know, and they are huge role models for young black kids everywhere. Basketball is really the only completely truly integrated sport. You'll see black and white players at every position—Chris Paul and Steve Nash at point guard, Durant and Kevin Love at forward, DeAndre Jordan and Marc Gasol at center, and the list goes on. At least half the coaches in the league are black, and a lot of executives, too. In football, it's starting to change with guys like Russell Wilson and Colin Kaepernick, but quarterback is still mostly a position for white stars. And around the rest of the field, your white guys are likely to be playing certain positions; black guys, others. Plus there aren't many minority coaches, even though there are plenty of qualified candidates.

Coming from where I'm coming from, race cuts through every angle of how I view sports. Golf is one of the few sports I'm not too interested in. If white people don't want me to join their clubs, then I don't want to play their game. Hockey's started to get a few more black players, including Seth Jones, Popeye Jones's son. But if hockey had as many black players as basketball does, fighting would have been outlawed twenty years ago. People are okay watching some white boys from Minnesota and Canada get in a tussle. But if black guys were throwing punches, the league and the fans wouldn't take it. I look at the American sports landscape, and I see that the predominantly black sports—football and basketball—are the sports that have age limits, all but require players to go to college, and have the most restrictive salary caps and limits on contract years.

The Donald Sterling fiasco during the 2014 playoffs demonstrated how integral race is in the NBA. The outrage over his comments completely overshadowed one of the most competitive first rounds ever for a weekend, before Adam Silver stepped in and basically threw Sterling out of the league. This incident made me recall how I thought the Clippers were going to draft me originally. That was before the lawsuits and stories came out about Sterling's being a slumlord and a racist, but I will say this: If I had been playing for the team when that started, I would have spoken up. As a league, I think we failed a bit in letting that guy stay around for so long. But when the issue exploded, you have to give Adam Silver credit for acting swiftly and strongly.

There's still progress to be made in basketball, though, as the controversy with the Atlanta Hawks a few months after the Sterling crisis made clear, with GM Danny Ferry exposed for saying disparaging words about Luol Deng in an internal meeting, and owner Bruce Levenson acknowledging that he himself had sent a racist e-mail. (Though, again, kudos to Commissioner Silver for again stepping in with a serious investigation, and soon after, the Hawks went up for sale.) Ultimately, around the NBA and the basketball media, if you dig deeply enough, you can identify a lot of subtle issues. Like when people complain about the AAU game hurting the development of players while praising international players as being more advanced. That kind of comment has a racial overtone to it. It's also ridiculous. Who's getting drafted first? The American players. Who's winning the international tournaments? The American players. End of conversation.

Race matters a lot to me because the color of my skin was a huge factor in how people viewed me from my first moments in the public eye at Michigan. If the Fab Five were white, everything would have been different.

Today, plenty of people in the media still don't know how to handle race. The same stereotypes and generalities are made. Andrew Luck is the "smart, resourceful" quarterback, while Russell Wilson is an "athletic marvel." LeBron James is the "best athlete in the NBA," while Larry Bird is a "basketball genius." It's frustrating when you know, as a fellow athlete, how talented and athletic Andrew Luck and Kevin Love are, and how smart Colin Kaepernick and LeBron James are.

It's why I'm gonna keep talking. Maybe someday they'll start listening.

12. Always Imperfect, Always Trying to Be Better, and How to Save the Ones Everyone Else Forgot About

If you get off the Lodge Freeway right before 8 Mile Road and make a turn onto Trojan Avenue, you can't miss it. It sits on the edge of Comstock Park, in what looks like a quiet neighborhood, even if nice, quiet neighborhoods aren't supposed to exist in Detroit anymore. From the outside, it looks like a lot of other schools. But inside those walls, what's going on is not happening almost anywhere else in the city.

The Jalen Rose Leadership Academy (JRLA) was opened in the fall of 2011. It's a tuition-free charter school, which means it's public (free, no admission tests—students are admitted through a lottery) but gets to determine its own curriculum, its own way of operating, and its own way of succeeding. It can raise outside money for additional funds, and get real commitments and financing from people willing to invest in the students and in the ideas espoused in the curriculum and the school philosophy. Charter schools have been growing across the country in troubled cities for a few decades now (something like 75 percent of schools in New Orleans are charters), and they make a lot of sense for a place like Detroit, where resources are a real problem and regular public schools therefore fall woefully short. People forget that when a city gets into trouble, the people impacted the most are children. As a city goes down, its schools go down with them. That leaves no hope at all for innocent victims who have little hope to begin with.

When I was a kid, I spent a lot of time frustrated about what I didn't have: no father, no money, no big house. Driving around Detroit today, all I can think of is what I did have: a fighting chance. A fighting chance, thanks to my mom and my uncles and then, later, my coaches and teachers, who didn't let me squander a golden opportunity to make it out, and make it big. On one of those drives I decided that once my playing days were over, my mission was going to be to help give that fighting chance to other kids through JRLA.

The school opened in 2011 with only 120 ninth graders. The next year, with those kids moving to tenth grade, a new crop of ninth graders came in. By the fall of 2014, we had four grades in the school, with our inaugural graduation—a landmark event—coming in the spring of 2015. Our goal is simple and non-negotiable: get 85 percent of our students to graduate, the same 85 percent of them to go to college, and the same 85 percent to graduate from college. And by the way, the average ninth grader comes into our school reading and doing math at a fifth-grade level.

JRLA is in the middle of northwest Detroit, in the same zip code that I grew up in. These days, almost any family that has a prayer of making it to the suburbs moves out of the city. They'll send their kids to live with relatives outside Detroit's borders. Our kids are the ones who couldn't make it out. Our kids are on that list of those that have been forgotten.

That's where the school comes in. We're giving these kids a fighting chance. They say it takes a village to raise a child—think of the school as the village. Or if you like a basketball analogy, think of me coaching a number sixteen seed in the tournament. We're supposed to have no chance to win.

But the most successful underdogs have something huge in common.

We all love it when everybody doubts us.

ONE OF the best things that ever happened to pro sports was when the players started getting paid. *Really* paid. For decades and decades, the individuals actually responsible for generating all the money around sports were paid far less than their value. Then free agency arrived—first in baseball and then in other sports, and suddenly the market began to talk. Combine that with the revolution in sports marketing and advertising, and you had Hall of Fame players like Magic and Michael turning themselves into Hall of Fame moguls. (Oh, Larry has got plenty of coin, too. Believe me. He just prefers a simpler life.)

Before this era, a lot of black sports stars were doing amazing things to bring attention to important issues, guys like Muhammad Ali, Bill Russell, Jim Brown, Arthur Ashe, John Carlos, and Tommie Smith. One of my favorite pictures was taken when Ali refused to go into the military, and he held a press conference in Cleveland. Russell, Jim Brown, and Kareem Abdul-Jabbar (then still Lew Alcindor) are sitting next to the Champ, with a whole bunch of other guys standing around behind them. The thing I appreciate about that picture is that those guys *had* to be socially and politically conscious, as the country was dealing with the realities of segregation. In the '60s, there were still Jim Crow laws, drinking out of different fountains, and all that. They stood up to say, "No! We're not three-fifths of a man. No! We're not second-class citizens. Yes, it's okay for us to have jobs and learn the English language." In a crazy time of upheaval and change, those guys didn't hesitate to put themselves right in the middle of everything.

So you'd think that once the successors to these stars became not just popular but rich, they'd find ways to have even more impact, right? Wrong. With the exception of Magic and AIDS, name one black superstar athlete of that generation or later who's made it a top priority to do something with his platform and bring real attention (and money) to a cause that means something to him. I can't think of any. The social and political conversation has gone away because the money is there, new opportunities are there, and so the sense of what the first superstars left behind is not at the top of their mind. Ultimately it comes down to the dollars. Let's face it, if you're an elite basketball player and you choose to be socially and politically active, it could harm your brand. As Michael Jordan said, "Republicans buy sneakers, too." I have no doubt that Michael—then and now—was proudly black, and had a mind to support minorities and the kinds of things that Democrats and liberals tend to support, but he knew that the Republicans were paying his bills, too.

Twenty years after Jordan, where are we now? Better off in some ways, and worse off in a lot of others. Guys today set up foundations and charities, and they give away a ton of money. But the truth is that way too few guys actually have their heart in it. They might write a check, but they don't pay attention to where it actually goes and where it could have the most impact. (Which means it might be going to some sham foundation, or some place that doesn't really know what it's doing.) The players show up at charity events because they have to, and they leave as soon as they can. If they're getting their minutes and their money, they don't pay attention to anyone else—not the fifteenth man on the bench, and certainly not those who are impacted when the government shuts down or there's a natural disaster.

We've got to be better than that—a lot better. So many players come from places that need help. Yes, change starts with money. If an athlete finds a cause, he's going to pour money into it. But also if he cares, he's going to bring attention to the issue, he's going to get others involved, and that's going to bring more money in, and round and round we go.

So how do we get there? We can't force athletes to give money away or to adopt a cause. We need to go back a step and do something even simpler: we need to find a way to get players to pay attention more. They have to look up and listen to what's going on around them, what's happening to their family members, what's happening to their friends back in the hood.

The NBA does a good job trying to get players involved, and that's been the case ever since the very first days of "NBA Cares." I think there's always room for growth, though. One idea I've had for a while is that fine money should be distributed to the charities of the player's choice. Right now, fine money gets put in a big pot that gets split between the league and the players union, and then distributed to a bunch of different charities and causes. That's a start, but I think it would be even better if the player, not the league, gets to choose where it's going. And there's a catch. The player would have to present the check to the organization in a public ceremony, and spend a day at that organization helping out. In the long run, maybe the player finds reasons to get involved, and brings some good publicity to those causes.

Small idea, but it's worth a shot.

I REMEMBER everything about growing up in Detroit. Eating big hamburgers at Yogi's. Ribs at Major's. Steve's Soul Food. Dot & Etta's Shrimp Hut. Days on the giant slide at Belle Isle, or the roller coaster at Edgewater Park. Taking the Bob-lo boat with all your friends. Nights out at the Dancery and Maxie's. Concerts at the State Theatre and Cobo Hall. Going to movies at the old Mercury Theatre and Norwest Theatre—I saw *Purple Rain* when it came out at the Norwest. Dreaming about trying to get on *The Scene,* our local answer to *Soul Train.* Buying records at the Hip Hop Shop. Getting gear at Strictly Sports. Then there was the high-end stuff—shopping at the Renaissance Center, with the Summit restaurant on top, slowly rotating around while people ate their dinners. The list goes on—the memories go on. When I grew up, Detroit was still thriving—and remembering that renews my faith in what the city can be.

I take pride in being socially and politically conscious. It all comes from the examples I had growing up. Uncle Paramore and Uncle Len, for starters. On top of the direct influence they had on keeping me straight, there was plenty else they did that made a mark. They suffered at their jobs, not getting promoted or getting the role they wanted because they were black, but they didn't just take it. They found ways to make it better for the next guy. Uncle P. became a foreman at the Ford plant, and everyone who worked at that factory with him has a story about how Paramore helped someone out, stood up for someone, or saved someone's job. Perry Watson continued that example, and so did Ed Martin.

These people cared about where they came from, which is why for me starting a school made sense. There is no better way to try and help who's coming up next in your community. We're not just trying to sneak a few kids into college by raising their test scores. It's called the Jalen Rose *Leadership* Academy for a reason—our goal is to *train leaders* for the next generation. Enter a learner, exit a leader—that's our motto. And there's a specialized curriculum and specialized training just for that. It all starts with the idea that there's no cutting corners. There's a rigorous college prep program and a continued focus on going to college. To accomplish all this, the kids are in school for eleven months a year, from 7:30 a.m. until after 4:00 p.m. Hiring teachers to work that long costs more money—and you need to find the best teachers for the jobs. We only have one sports team, too—you can guess the sport. And Curtis Hervey, my old AAU coach, runs our basketball program. So I know that team's in good hands.

Just like the kids, JRLA has got pretty much everything going against it. A lot of our kids don't have Internet at home, and their parents don't have e-mail addresses. We keep the kids off the streets until 4:00, but often their parents can't pick them up until 5:30 or 6:30 because they can't get off work. They aren't ignoring their kids. They have no choice. Also, almost none of our ninth graders arrive reading and doing math at grade level. But that's the age we decided to tackle—the age where you can lock kids in for college, which will lock them into all kinds of opportunities. We try to do everything we can to get these kids into college.

If we were a school outside of the city, we'd get twice as much money per kid than we do. We get $7,700 per kid per year, as of right now—and just outside the city, they get more than $12,000. Plus, there are bigger charter networks in Detroit that are better funded and bigger causes—the University of Michigan, hospitals, whatever—that draw far more attention when people decide to open their checkbooks. Places like that routinely get six- and seven-figure gifts. For us, a five-figure gift is a huge deal.

We've been fortunate to have some huge benefactors. Tom Gores—owner of the Pistons and founder of Platinum Equity—and his wife, Holly, have been huge. Chrysler Jeep stepped up, which was significant, considering my mom's job there all those years ago. The Lear Corporation. And there have been NBA players and coaches and franchises who have contributed, Hall of Famers like my mentor Dave Bing, and Isiah and Lynn Thomas. Kobe even let me out of that hex from the Finals all those years ago and donated shoes to all the kids in the school. There are dozens of others who've stepped up as well, for the most basic things—carpet, paint, pens, pencils, paper, you name it.

The goal for the school is to turn ourselves from a number sixteen seed to a midmajor. We probably won't be the biggest powerhouse in the bracket, but we want to be a school that people know is going to be there, battle hard, and have the resources to do so.

We'll get there. Because I'm not going to accept anything else.

. . .

I FOUNDED a school because I determined it was the best way to help kids in my hometown in a significant, meaningful way. But I also think a lot about different struggles that young people from less fortunate backgrounds face all over the country. I joke on my podcast about champagning and campaigning and the gangsta life, but it's important to confront the realities of what these kids from the inner cities are up against.

Why do kids join gangs? The number one reason: They can't move away from them. In my day, gangsters left nongangsters alone. Now, if you live in South Central Los Angeles, you probably don't have the means to move anywhere else. So the gang is your block, and eventually you have to join them or get treated like the enemy. You have no option. Most people who live that lifestyle are not doing so because they want to; they have to.

Being trapped in that environment shapes everything about you. Including how you present yourself. If you walk around with your pants low, showing your underwear, that influences how you will be viewed. When I did that, I sometimes used to think that my appearance made me tough. Like I was rough-and-tumble. Now I realize that all it means was that I had my pants down. "Saggin'" spelled backwards is not a way of life to aspire to.

If you have a tattoo on your neck or your face, it will be noticed at a job interview. Regardless of what is right or wrong, beyond the sports world, the music world, and the entertainment world, people in power in corporate America have no interest in the hip-hop life-style or look. Studies say 65 percent of communication is nonverbal. Your wardrobe, your hygiene, and your presentation are a huge part of how you are perceived. And being a minority in everything puts you in a position where you sometimes need to conform to be accepted.

Those are just facts. Facts surrounding a serious uphill climb for less fortunate people in our country, many of whom are black. It ain't easy. But that's never been a good excuse.

YOU CAN'T go back in time. Mistakes are what shape you, missteps are what you learn from, and misfires are what make you focus harder the next time. But there's definitely one regret, one failure, that still haunts me almost every morning I get up, and almost every night when I go to sleep. It's really the biggest reason that back in 2007, when I sat there at Jimmy Walker's funeral, I was full of fear. It has nothing to do with basketball, and nothing to do with my job today.

It's that my kids live thousands of miles away from me, in another city, and that means I can't be the dad that I want to be for them.

Really, it haunts me to write that, because my own history is part of an epidemic in the NBA, in sports, and in African American culture. I came from the seed of a man who had, they say, thirteen kids by eleven women. I played with some teammates who had almost as many. I was in the middle of the lifestyle that fosters this kind of behavior, and this kind of consequence. But the idea that "lifestyle" forces players to father kids all over the place is a bunch of bull.

Believe me, in my years in the NBA, I was familiar with the math that the late, great Wilt Chamberlain did to get the numbers he came up with. They were more accurate than you think. But in all my travels, in all the cities, I never made one mistake. I told you as a rookie, I used to have to go on jimmy hat runs for the vets? Well, I was always smart enough to pick up Magnums for myself as well, and I helped keep the good people at Trojan in business, and then some, throughout my career. It's total bull when you hear a guy say that a girl tricked him, or took advantage of him. Everyone—and certainly every NBA player—knows exactly what's up, and where and when everything is going to finish. Which means it's the player's fault when a pregnancy happens by accident, and a child comes into the world who isn't going to grow up with a father around.

I tried to do everything I could to avoid that scenario. But the fact is that two things I never wanted—to have kids and not be married, and to live in another city than my kids do—are my reality. My older daughter was born right after we went to the Finals in Indiana—just as I was preparing to settle there for the long term with my long-term girlfriend. I bought a big house for us and our family. But then things went south between us, and we broke up. Since we weren't married, when my girlfriend took our daughter with her out of town, the law left me no options. And so less than a year after my daughter was born, I had exactly what I didn't want: a child living hundreds of miles away from me.

When I got traded anyway, I decided never to buy another house in another city I played in ever again. Several years later, during a brief reconciliation with my ex, we had another daughter. That's left me with the best two blessings in my life living as sisters with their mom. I parachute in monthly (definitely not enough during the season, and still not enough in the off-season) to go to games and concerts, to carpool, and to participate in other school events as they grow up way too quickly. I try to make it as normal as possible.

It's not the kind of father I want to be, but I do know that I do everything I can to be as good of a dad as I can under the circumstances. Still, all in all, it sucks to be an out-of-town dad.

It's interesting to have debates about this issue with people who don't come from places where absentee dads are common. When the topic of pro athletes having kids out of wedlock and out of one-night stands comes up, they make the point that a player who has tens of millions of dollars in the bank can support a kid, no problem. Well, I'd like to remind you that I'm evidence that it's not always no problem. If not for men like Sam Washington and Perry Watson, I'd just be a tall black guy now living in Detroit insisting to everyone that I could have been a star. Fathers who aren't with mothers disappear. And their checks disappear as well. Yeah, it's a little different now in a world with the Internet and social media, but when a kid grows up, the first thing he or she realizes is when a parent doesn't want them. That's damaging, no matter if the money is there or not.

I've tried to do as much as I could with my own imperfect predicament. It's not always easy to coparent with someone you are not married to, but together, we do our best to work through it. My ex is a great mom, and ultimately, my most important goal is that my daughters have a better life than I did, and they get in a position to fulfill all their hopes and dreams. They live in a gated community, they go to an amazing private school, and they are going to have a great shot at a successful life doing whatever they want to do. I hope my girls know that even though their mom and I aren't married, I will always do the right thing. And that includes supporting their brother. You see, the mother of my daughters already had a son when we met. And, go figure, the boy's father was a professional athlete from Michigan who'd disappeared from the picture after the two of them broke up. If you're a sports fan of a certain age, you'll remember him—former NFL wide receiver Andre Rison. I normally don't call people out like this, but in this situation, I have no hesitations, if only to shine a spotlight on what his son has done with his life. He is now in his early twenties, and after going to Holy Cross on a full scholarship, he got a graduate degree in economics at Imperial College London, and still works there. Though I was not there at his birth, I have considered him my son since the day I met him, and began supporting him. He's a member of my family.

Like Mos Def said, though, I ain't no perfect man. Sixteen days a few summers ago definitely reminded me of that, and then some.

ASIDE FROM the crack house incident, and I guess the time in Beverly Hills when my car got shot at, if you googled me, you wouldn't find anything negative. At least until a snowy night in Detroit in 2011—when I almost blew everything I'd built.

The moral of the story is pretty simple: don't drink and drive. That may sound simple and obvious, but read the sentence again—don't drink and drive. That doesn't mean don't drive when you're drunk—it means, if you've had one drink, don't get behind the wheel of a car. It's dumb—and also outdated. Driving after you've been drinking is like still having a SkyPager. You now have a plethora of choices. Wherever I am, I'm a car service's best friend.

But on that night, right around when the Fab Five documentary was coming out, I was driving home after a night out. On the icy road, a few miles from my house, I pulled out of a light, skidded across the road, and ended up in a ditch on the side of the road. A second later, a guy taps on my window to check on me. I was okay, but—as fate would have it—he was an undercover cop, and a minute later, there were sirens everywhere. Again, I didn't feel drunk, but as I'd soon be reminded, that didn't matter. The Breathalyzer said I was over the limit, and that meant there wasn't going to be any fighting it.

A few weeks later, I found out the judge who was hearing my case felt that, no matter who you are, if you drink and drive, you do time. Which led to me serving sixteen days in jail that summer (a twenty-day sentence . . . I got four days off for good behavior). And, look—since fortunately nobody got hurt or killed—that was a pretty light punishment for something so dumb.

ESPN was great—they supported me, they listened to my side of it, and they didn't fire me. And for two weeks in county jail, I did the only thing I could think to do: make the best of it. I got one of those jobs they give you, cleaning out cells and distributing food. I got to know some of the people serving time. Hopefully, hanging out with someone who they recognized, who like them had been humbled a bit, was good for them.

Then, in a twist of fate I cannot explain, a familiar face was brought in to be my cellmate for the last few days of my sentence: Jimmy King. He'd fallen behind on his child support payments and had to do a short sentence. My old teammate—my brother— alongside me, there for each other at a tough moment for each of us.

A reminder that none of us is perfect.

A reminder that you're going to mess up a few times here and there.

And then you go back to the task of winning the game of life.

. . .

PAYING ATTENTION to trends has always been important to me. New acts in hip-hop. New styles in fashion. New stars coming up the ranks in basketball. That's what I was doing a few years ago when I saw that *Grantland* was going to be the next big thing in sports media. I had been following Bill Simmons and reading his columns for a long time, and my ears perked up when he was able to get ESPN to give him own website, Grantland.com.

I enjoyed what I was doing—studio analysis on the NBA and occasionally college basketball—but I wanted to be doing more. Appreciate your position, but plan your promotion. I wanted to be talking about other sports. I wanted to contribute to *ESPN The Magazine* and ESPN.com. But I wasn't getting much traction on those fronts.

Grantland was something different. And it was being established in Los Angeles, literally a ten-minute drive from where I live. So I monitored it a bit, got a sense of what was going on, and then, at the ESPY Awards that summer, made sure I was at the party where Bill was going to be, and I went up to him and talked to him—the first time we'd really met. I told him what a big fan I was, not just of his writing, but also his work on his podcast. And then I told him I wanted to pitch him ideas for his new site. I think if you asked him today, he'd admit that he gave me a look that said, *Really? You want to pitch me ideas about the site?* But I was serious, and I got his e-mail address, and I e-mailed him the very next day.

When we got together a few weeks later, I knew exactly what I wanted to do: a podcast that would be like an old-school radio show, back-and-forth talking about sports, music, culture, anything and everything that was in the news. But I also knew I needed a partner. I had my eye on exactly the man I wanted: Bill's producer and friend David Jacoby, who had been appearing on Bill's podcast for years. Bill was a little skeptical, saying that Jacoby was busy and had his hands full with the launch of the site, but the two of us could talk about it and figure out if it was possible.

Of course it was possible.

Now our podcast gets hundreds of thousands of hits on iTunes and YouTube, and we've also expanded it with the NBA video pods I do with Bill before and during the season, which mesh well with my work on *NBA Countdown* and other shows on ESPN that I'm involved in. It all goes back to what I started with back in Detroit all those years ago: I'm competitive and want to be the best. And while TNT still gets a lot of the plaudits (and sure, they deserve them), those guys aren't nearly as involved on as many platforms and as many forums as we are. And that's not just the future—it's the present. It could well be how you came to this book—after hearing or watching one of our podcasts. They've become my favorite thing to do in my media career. Yes, the network is the bigger audience, but the podcasts allow me to be myself in every way possible. And I feel like the audience recognizes that.

It's very simple—you've got to give the people what they want.

WHENEVER I see Steph Curry, I joke with him about the same thing. At some point within the next few seasons, he's going to pass the 12,000-point mark, and a few weeks after that, he's going to pass the only NBA record I hold. Well, I share it. Most points scored by a father and son in league history (with each player having at least 10,000 points—sorry, Kobe and Jellybean Bryant). I had 13,220, and Jimmy Walker had 11,655. (And don't forget— Jimmy played before the three-point line was instituted.) Steph and his father, Dell Curry, already have passed the 20,000 mark, and obviously Steph is coming on strong. I know it's just a footnote to everyone else, but for me, it's a symbol of what I accomplished— and kind of the perfect summation of my feelings for my father. I wanted to be like him, but did so in spite of him. I always wanted him to know my name, and I was able to get our names connected in the best place possible: the record book. Today, I root for Providence, his alma mater. An old friend of mine, Mike Jackson, who I played against in eighth grade, is an assistant coach there.

There are other small legacies I hold on to in basketball. Being one of the few six-foot-eight point guards to come through the league— an elite club that includes Magic Johnson, Steve Smith, and Penny Hardaway. I may not have been able to copy Steve's hesitation dribble and keep that move alive—but I did emulate him by getting from Detroit to the league. And we root for big point guards like Shaun Livingston who are playing today. There's also the legion of left-handed number 5s who've played in the NBA: Lamar Odom, Cuttino Mobley, Josh Smith—and a handful of others in college ball.

But even if not too many people thumb through stats or categorize players like that, there is another way I've carved out a legacy, in basketball and beyond, that I'm proud of. I don't think my mom realized what she was starting when she decided to create a new name that winter night I was born, but she laid the groundwork for a phenomenon. I'm serious—I don't use that word lightly. Remember I told you at the beginning of the book how my Uncle Len was surprised to hear a mom yelling for her son—"Jalen!"—in a mall in

Detroit? Well, it went far beyond that mall, and far beyond Detroit.
They've been tracking name data in the United States going back to
1880, and in the early 1990s, when the Fab Five hit, "Jalen" became
the hottest name in history. No other name had a bigger jump in
popularity, ever. Today, many people, former teammates of mine
like Rick Brunson and Eddie Robinson, have sons named Jalen.
Dr. J himself, Julius Erving, has a grandson named Jalen. People
sometimes spell it with a *y* or other differences. Mike Miller has
a daughter named Jaelyn. Of all the trends I follow, this one's my
favorite. Because when people name their kid after you, it's not just
that they like the sound of the name. It's that they appreciate who
that name is associated with, and what it represents.

As crazy as it might sound, I view that as a responsibility. To
keep moving forward, to keep winning the game of life, to keep
doing things that matter wherever the journey takes me. As a player,
I was in the middle of a team that transformed basketball and its
relationship to culture and society. With the microphone, I'm doing
everything I can to transform how the media can change your per-
ception of sports and of athletes. And we're still only getting started
with JRLA in Detroit. I've got other commitments I'm excited about
as well. I'm an official ambassador now of the National Basketball
Retired Players Association (NBRPA), working to assist current and
former players in their lives after the game, and in serving communities. I'm also an ambassador for the American Federation for
Children, and am on the board of directors of StudentsFirst, both of
which are tied in to educational causes on a national level.

My goal—my vow—is never to change, and never to be ashamed
of who I am, or who I was. If we went out to play pickup right now,

believe me, I will talk trash the whole time, get in your head, do what I can to beat you. (Though—if you've noticed over the last two hundred pages—I won't swear. My mom heard me swearing one night when she was at a game late in my career, and scolded me for it. So I made everything PG-rated from then on. She was right. No need to use bad words when the good ones give you plenty of material.)

I'm gonna keep talking about the Fab Five because I think our legacy is important, and what we stood for and represented was important. Nothing makes me prouder than to hear during the 2014 Final Four that the Kentucky players—with all freshmen in the starting five—were fans of the Fab Five, and had watched the documentary before the tournament. They weren't even alive when we made our runs. But they recognized the roots of what they were accomplishing.

What's next? Well, for one thing, I want that happy ending. Growing up in the hood, you don't realize the kind of happy ending you deserve. I want to get married, I want to have more kids, and decades from now, I want to have grandkids. I want another generation to be part of the annual family reunions at my mom's house every summer. Where my ninety-seven-year-old grandmother still makes sure everyone is doing the right thing. Where Uncle Len and Uncle Paramore still hold court—they've battled some health problems but are still two of the strongest men I know. Bill and Kev and Tam are there, too—with their own spouses and kids. Bill works at a bank, and he and his wife have twin daughters, Courtney and Chelsea. Kev's retired from the service, with a big family, too. And Tam has two kids of her own, also. Everyone's doing well.

And when I look in the mirror, and see a kid who once looked up to gangsters like Butch Jones and the YBIs—I realize how lucky I am, and how badly I want that luck to continue.

What else? I'd love to run a team someday. Either in the NBA as a general manager, or in the college ranks coaching a program. And I also dream about becoming a minority owner of my home-town Pistons. We've seen a whole bunch of individuals in the media make the transition to those kinds of jobs, and we've seen them suc-ceed. It's a natural progression. In the pros, I know better than ever why teams win and why teams lose, and how good players become great, and how great players become legends. In college, I guarantee you there'd be no better recruiter—no one better to help these kids to deal with the difficulty of college basketball, the ridiculousness of the NCAA, and the unbelievable things that can happen when you dominate the game. I've talked to people out there, and they know I'm interested. So just be ready if it happens. I came up one step short of a title in both the pros and the NCAA. It would be a perfect reason to go back, and finish what I started.

Hey, doubt me if you want.

Because you know there's nothing I love more than proving the doubters wrong.

THE TAO OF JALEN: A GUIDE TO WINNING THE GAME OF LIFE

1. **Encourage your doubters.** They don't think you belong. Let that be the fuel that vaults you past them.

2. **Do your research.** It applies to trash-talking, and it applies to life. Nothing better than surprising someone about what you know. It's a signal you have more surprises coming.

3. **Play hard. Work harder.** Champagning and campaigning is one of the world's oldest and greatest pastimes. But the only players who matter are the ones who did more work than you think to get the table behind the velvet rope.

4. **Speak up. Just because someone's in charge doesn't mean your job is to always listen to them.** Be respectful, but smart challenges to authority earn you more respect than you might think.

5. **Love life. It can be easy to focus on the things that frustrate you.** But the blessings will get you up earlier in the morning, keep you going later at night, and always keep you on the lookout for more.

ACKNOWLEDGMENTS

I'll start out these acknowledgments by saying that this entire book is an acknowledgment. Every person mentioned on these pages played a role in the road I've traveled to this point. I have such tremendous gratitude for all of my family and friends—especially my brothers Bill and Kevin, and my sister Tammy. Thank you for the love, support, and game! I definitely can't forget my Aunt Jackie, who was a teacher and stressed the importance of education and challenged me not to be a dumb jock.

Thank you to my Lord and Savior Jesus Christ . . . Psalm 23!

Endless love to my amazing children: LaDarius, Mariah, and Gracie. I have the best kids that any father could have. Your intelligence, hard work, and discipline are unmatched. Please keep God first and continue to sacrifice for your dreams. I love you! Special thanks also to Mauri, who is an amazing mom.

Next, Krissy. My queen, boss, and therapist. Thank you for loving me unconditionally and allowing me to be your Knight in Shining Armor.

I want to thank Aaron Cohen for making this book possible. Aaron and I first met in New York to discuss *The Fab Five* documentary in the fall of 2010. The connection was instant, and he became a huge part of the success of the film. Writing a book was a huge challenge, but Aaron was the perfect guy to help me tell my story. Big ups to AC.

I had always wanted to write a book, but Daniel Greenberg of LGR Literary was the guy to come up with the right pitch. He teamed up with Cait Hoyt and my guy Nick Khan at CAA, and we were on our way. Special shout-out to Nick, the best agent in the business.

Mary Choteborsky at Penguin Random House did an incredible job editing the book, along with assists from Nathan Roberson and Julia Elliott.

I'm truly grateful to have the best executive assistant and friend, Michelle Ruscitti-Miller, who has kept me on point for over a decade. And I can't forget my business manager, David Bolno, and his NKSFB staff, who see to it that my dollars make sense. Teamwork is making dreams work!

Much love to David Jacoby and Bill Simmons for supporting the project, and of course, to Bill for writing the foreword—good luck at HBO!

And last but not least, you—the fans—for making Jalen one of the most popular names around the world. Thank you for supporting *The Rose That Grew from Concrete* since day one. "I'm waaay up. I feel BLESSED" (Big Sean).